Homeschool Pl

MW00465924

& RECORD BOOK

THIS PLANNER BELONGS TO

TO

DATE

DATE

NAME

GRADE

This Homeschool Planner is designed to help you organize the curriculum and records for one to three students. It is undated, allowing you to begin anytime. Set goals and stay on track with weekly, monthly, and yearly planning prompts.

Make lesson plans and document the progress of your children with up to 12 months of tracking subjects, assignments, projects, grades, attendance, and more. Includes a dedicated place to list important contacts, your accounts, passwords, and the events/field trips you are planning for the year. There are recap/notes pages at the end of each week and each month, pages for brainstorming and additional notes at the end of the book so you can plan more effectively next year. Consider purchasing tabs as they are great for indexing, and they allow for quick access to frequently used pages.

Homeschooling is a serious and honorable endeavor. This planner is designed to help you succeed as you educate your children and prepare them for success.

Table of Contents

Contacts

Name	Contact Information

Account Tracker

Account Name	Purchased Date	Expire/ Renewal	Price

Password Tracker

Website/Account	Username/ Login	Password	Notes

Our Year At A Glance

Important Dates

FEBRUARY

MARCH

APRIL

MAY

JUNE

JULY

GOAL		ACHIEVED
# of weeks _____		# of weeks _____
# of days _____	7	# of days _____

YEARLY SUBJECT *Planner*

Subject	Goal	Required Resource

Name:

Subject	Goal	Required Resource

Name:

Subject	Goal	Required Resource

Name:

YEARLY CURRICULUM *Planner*

Budget: _____

Name:	Subject	Curriculum/Supplies	Cost
		Total	

Name:	Subject	Curriculum/Supplies	Cost
		Total	

Name:	Subject	Curriculum/Supplies	Cost
		Total	

Grand Total _____

UNITED STATES FEDERAL HOLIDAYS & OBSERVANCES

January 1	New Year's Day	3rd Sunday in June	Father's Day
3rd Monday in January	Martin Luther King Day	July 4	Independence Day
January 23	National Pie Day	4th Sunday of July	Parent's Day
January 24	Global Belly Laugh Day	August 8	National CBD Day
February 1	National Freedom Day	August 19	National Aviation Day
February 2	Groundhog Day	1st Monday in September	Labor Day
February 9	National Pizza Day	1st Sunday after Labor Day	National Grandparent's Day
February 12	Lincoln's Birthday	September 11	Patriot Day
February 14	Valentine's Day	September 16	Stepfamily Day
3rd Monday in February	President's Day & Washington's Birthday	September 17	Constitution Day & Citizenship Day
March 17	St. Patrick's Day	3rd Friday of September	National POW/MIA Recognition Day
March 29	National Vietnam War Veterans Day	4th Friday of September	Native American Day
April 1	April Fool's Day	September 29	National Coffee Day
April 7	National Beer Day	2nd Monday in October	Columbus Day
April 13	Thomas Jefferson's Birthday	October 16	Boss's Day
April 15	Tax Day	3rd Saturday of October	Sweetest Day
April 22	Earth Day	October 31	Halloween
1st Thursday of May	National Day of Prayer	1st Tuesday of November	Election Day
2nd Sunday in May	Mother's Day	November 11	Veteran's Day
May 5	Cinco de Mayo	4th Thursday of the month	Thanksgiving
May 15	Peace Officers Memorial Day	December 7	Pearl Harbor Remembrance Day
3rd Saturday in May	Armed Forces Day	December 17	Wright Brother's Day
May 22	National Maritime Day	December 25	Christmas Day
1st Thursday in May	National Day of Prayer	December 31	New Year's Eve
1st Friday in June	National Donut Day		

10

MONTH _____   YEAR _____

SUNDAY	MONDAY	TUESDAY	WEDNESDAY

It takes a BIG HEART to teach little minds

THURSDAY	FRIDAY	SATURDAY	REMINDERS/NOTES
			○ _____ _____ _____ _____
			○ _____ _____ _____
			○ _____ _____
			○ _____ _____ _____
			○ _____ _____ ○ _____ _____ _____ _____

Weekly Plan

Week of _____

TO DO'S/*Notes*

_____
_____
_____
_____
_____
_____
_____
_____
_____
_____
_____

_____
_____
_____
_____
_____
_____
_____
_____
_____
_____
_____

Goals

Projects

14

It takes a BIG HEART to teach little minds

THURSDAY	FRIDAY	SATURDAY	REMINDERS/NOTES
			○ _____ _____ _____ _____
			○ _____ _____ _____
			○ _____ _____ _____
			○ _____ _____ _____
			○ _____ ○ _____ _____ _____ _____

Weekly Plan

Week of _____

TO DO'S/*Notes*

_____
_____
_____
_____
_____
_____
_____
_____
_____
_____

_____
_____
_____
_____
_____
_____
_____
_____
_____
_____

Goals

Projects

Weekly Curriculum Plan

Week of _____

<table>
<tr><td>MATH</td><td>NAME</td><td>MONDAY</td><td>TUESDAY</td><td>WEDNESDAY</td><td>THURSDAY</td><td>FRIDAY</td></tr>
</table>

MATH	NAME	MONDAY	TUESDAY	WEDNESDAY	THURSDAY	FRIDAY

SCIENCE	NAME	MONDAY	TUESDAY	WEDNESDAY	THURSDAY	FRIDAY

HISTORY	NAME	MONDAY	TUESDAY	WEDNESDAY	THURSDAY	FRIDAY

ENGLISH	NAME	MONDAY	TUESDAY	WEDNESDAY	THURSDAY	FRIDAY

NAME	MONDAY	TUESDAY	WEDNESDAY	THURSDAY	FRIDAY

NAME	MONDAY	TUESDAY	WEDNESDAY	THURSDAY	FRIDAY

NAME	MONDAY	TUESDAY	WEDNESDAY	THURSDAY	FRIDAY

NAME	MONDAY	TUESDAY	WEDNESDAY	THURSDAY	FRIDAY

Weekly ASSIGNMENTS

Week of _____

Name:	○	○
	○	○
	○	○
	○	○

Name:	○	○
	○	○
	○	○
	○	○

Name:	○	○
	○	○
	○	○
	○	○

Videos WATCHED

Name:

Name:

Name:

Brainstorm

Weekly Plan

Week of _____

TO DO'S/*Notes*

_____
_____
_____
_____
_____
_____
_____
_____
_____
_____

_____
_____
_____
_____
_____
_____
_____
_____
_____
_____

Goals

Projects

Weekly Curriculum Plan

Week of _____

	NAME	MONDAY	TUESDAY	WEDNESDAY	THURSDAY	FRIDAY
MATH						

	NAME	MONDAY	TUESDAY	WEDNESDAY	THURSDAY	FRIDAY
SCIENCE						

	NAME	MONDAY	TUESDAY	WEDNESDAY	THURSDAY	FRIDAY
HISTORY						

	NAME	MONDAY	TUESDAY	WEDNESDAY	THURSDAY	FRIDAY
ENGLISH						

NAME	MONDAY	TUESDAY	WEDNESDAY	THURSDAY	FRIDAY

NAME	MONDAY	TUESDAY	WEDNESDAY	THURSDAY	FRIDAY

NAME	MONDAY	TUESDAY	WEDNESDAY	THURSDAY	FRIDAY

NAME	MONDAY	TUESDAY	WEDNESDAY	THURSDAY	FRIDAY

Weekly ASSIGNMENTS

Week of _____

Name:	○	○
	○	○
	○	○
	○	○

Name:	○	○
	○	○
	○	○
	○	○

Name:	○	○
	○	○
	○	○
	○	○

Videos WATCHED

Name:

Name:

Name:

Brainstorm

Weekly Plan

Week of _____

TO DO'S/*Notes*

_____
_____
_____
_____
_____
_____
_____
_____
_____
_____

_____
_____
_____
_____
_____
_____
_____
_____
_____
_____

Goals

Projects

22

Weekly Curriculum Plan

Week of _____

<table>
<tr><td rowspan="5" style="writing-mode: vertical-lr">MATH</td></tr>
<tr><th>NAME</th><th>MONDAY</th><th>TUESDAY</th><th>WEDNESDAY</th><th>THURSDAY</th><th>FRIDAY</th></tr>
<tr><td></td><td></td><td></td><td></td><td></td><td></td></tr>
<tr><td></td><td></td><td></td><td></td><td></td><td></td></tr>
<tr><td></td><td></td><td></td><td></td><td></td><td></td></tr>
</table>

SCIENCE	NAME	MONDAY	TUESDAY	WEDNESDAY	THURSDAY	FRIDAY

HISTORY	NAME	MONDAY	TUESDAY	WEDNESDAY	THURSDAY	FRIDAY

ENGLISH	NAME	MONDAY	TUESDAY	WEDNESDAY	THURSDAY	FRIDAY

	NAME	MONDAY	TUESDAY	WEDNESDAY	THURSDAY	FRIDAY

	NAME	MONDAY	TUESDAY	WEDNESDAY	THURSDAY	FRIDAY

	NAME	MONDAY	TUESDAY	WEDNESDAY	THURSDAY	FRIDAY

	NAME	MONDAY	TUESDAY	WEDNESDAY	THURSDAY	FRIDAY

Weekly ASSIGNMENTS

Week of _____

Name:	○		○	
	○		○	
	○		○	
	○		○	

Name:	○		○	
	○		○	
	○		○	
	○		○	

Name:	○		○	
	○		○	
	○		○	
	○		○	

Videos WATCHED

Name:

Name:

Name:

Brainstorm

Weekly Plan

Week of _____

TO DO'S/*Notes*

_____
_____
_____
_____
_____
_____
_____
_____
_____
_____

_____
_____
_____
_____
_____
_____
_____
_____
_____
_____

Goals

Projects

Weekly Curriculum Plan

Week of _____

	NAME	MONDAY	TUESDAY	WEDNESDAY	THURSDAY	FRIDAY
MATH						

	NAME	MONDAY	TUESDAY	WEDNESDAY	THURSDAY	FRIDAY
SCIENCE						

	NAME	MONDAY	TUESDAY	WEDNESDAY	THURSDAY	FRIDAY
HISTORY						

	NAME	MONDAY	TUESDAY	WEDNESDAY	THURSDAY	FRIDAY
ENGLISH						

NAME	MONDAY	TUESDAY	WEDNESDAY	THURSDAY	FRIDAY

NAME	MONDAY	TUESDAY	WEDNESDAY	THURSDAY	FRIDAY

NAME	MONDAY	TUESDAY	WEDNESDAY	THURSDAY	FRIDAY

NAME	MONDAY	TUESDAY	WEDNESDAY	THURSDAY	FRIDAY

Weekly ASSIGNMENTS

Week of _____

Name:	○		○	
	○		○	
	○		○	
	○		○	

Name:	○		○	
	○		○	
	○		○	
	○		○	

Name:	○		○	
	○		○	
	○		○	
	○		○	

Videos WATCHED

Name:

Name:

Name:

Brainstorm

Monthly Reading Register

STUDENT:

Book Title & Author:
○ _____
○ _____
○ _____

STUDENT:

Book Title & Author:
○ _____
○ _____
○ _____

STUDENT:

Book Title & Author:
○ _____
○ _____
○ _____

Monthly Recap & Notes

MONTH   YEAR

SUNDAY	MONDAY	TUESDAY	WEDNESDAY

It takes a BIG HEART to teach little minds

THURSDAY	FRIDAY	SATURDAY	REMINDERS/NOTES
			○ _____ _____ _____ _____
			○ _____ _____ _____ _____
			○ _____ _____ _____ _____
			○ _____ _____ _____ _____
			○ _____ _____ _____ ○ _____ _____ _____ _____

Weekly Plan

Week of _____

TO DO'S/Notes

_____
_____
_____
_____
_____
_____
_____
_____
_____

_____
_____
_____
_____
_____
_____
_____
_____
_____

Goals

Projects

Weekly Curriculum Plan

Week of _____

	NAME	MONDAY	TUESDAY	WEDNESDAY	THURSDAY	FRIDAY
MATH						

	NAME	MONDAY	TUESDAY	WEDNESDAY	THURSDAY	FRIDAY
SCIENCE						

	NAME	MONDAY	TUESDAY	WEDNESDAY	THURSDAY	FRIDAY
HISTORY						

	NAME	MONDAY	TUESDAY	WEDNESDAY	THURSDAY	FRIDAY
ENGLISH						

NAME	MONDAY	TUESDAY	WEDNESDAY	THURSDAY	FRIDAY

NAME	MONDAY	TUESDAY	WEDNESDAY	THURSDAY	FRIDAY

NAME	MONDAY	TUESDAY	WEDNESDAY	THURSDAY	FRIDAY

NAME	MONDAY	TUESDAY	WEDNESDAY	THURSDAY	FRIDAY

Weekly ASSIGNMENTS

Week of _____

Name:	○	○
	○	○
	○	○
	○	○

Name:	○	○
	○	○
	○	○
	○	○

Name:	○	○
	○	○
	○	○
	○	○

Videos WATCHED

Name:

Name:

Name:

Brainstorm

Weekly Plan

Week of _____

TO DO'S/Notes

_____
_____
_____
_____
_____
_____
_____
_____
_____

_____
_____
_____
_____
_____
_____
_____
_____
_____
_____

Goals

Projects

Weekly Curriculum Plan

Week of _____

<table>
<tr><td rowspan="2">MATH</td><td>NAME</td><td>MONDAY</td><td>TUESDAY</td><td>WEDNESDAY</td><td>THURSDAY</td><td>FRIDAY</td></tr>
<tr><td></td><td></td><td></td><td></td><td></td><td></td></tr>
</table>

MATH	NAME	MONDAY	TUESDAY	WEDNESDAY	THURSDAY	FRIDAY

SCIENCE	NAME	MONDAY	TUESDAY	WEDNESDAY	THURSDAY	FRIDAY

HISTORY	NAME	MONDAY	TUESDAY	WEDNESDAY	THURSDAY	FRIDAY

ENGLISH	NAME	MONDAY	TUESDAY	WEDNESDAY	THURSDAY	FRIDAY

NAME	MONDAY	TUESDAY	WEDNESDAY	THURSDAY	FRIDAY

NAME	MONDAY	TUESDAY	WEDNESDAY	THURSDAY	FRIDAY

NAME	MONDAY	TUESDAY	WEDNESDAY	THURSDAY	FRIDAY

NAME	MONDAY	TUESDAY	WEDNESDAY	THURSDAY	FRIDAY

Weekly ASSIGNMENTS

Week of _____

Name:	○		○	
	○		○	
	○		○	
	○		○	

Name:	○		○	
	○		○	
	○		○	
	○		○	

Name:	○		○	
	○		○	
	○		○	
	○		○	

Videos WATCHED

Name:

Name:

Name:

Brainstorm

Weekly Plan

Week of _____

TO DO'S/*Notes*

_____

_____

_____

_____

_____

_____

_____

_____

_____

_____

_____

_____

_____

_____

_____

_____

_____

_____

_____

_____

_____

Goals

Projects

Weekly Curriculum Plan

Week of _____

<table>
<tr><td rowspan="4">MATH</td><td>NAME</td><td>MONDAY</td><td>TUESDAY</td><td>WEDNESDAY</td><td>THURSDAY</td><td>FRIDAY</td></tr>
<tr><td></td><td></td><td></td><td></td><td></td><td></td></tr>
<tr><td></td><td></td><td></td><td></td><td></td><td></td></tr>
<tr><td></td><td></td><td></td><td></td><td></td><td></td></tr>
</table>

<table>
<tr><td rowspan="4">SCIENCE</td><td>NAME</td><td>MONDAY</td><td>TUESDAY</td><td>WEDNESDAY</td><td>THURSDAY</td><td>FRIDAY</td></tr>
<tr><td></td><td></td><td></td><td></td><td></td><td></td></tr>
<tr><td></td><td></td><td></td><td></td><td></td><td></td></tr>
<tr><td></td><td></td><td></td><td></td><td></td><td></td></tr>
</table>

<table>
<tr><td rowspan="4">HISTORY</td><td>NAME</td><td>MONDAY</td><td>TUESDAY</td><td>WEDNESDAY</td><td>THURSDAY</td><td>FRIDAY</td></tr>
<tr><td></td><td></td><td></td><td></td><td></td><td></td></tr>
<tr><td></td><td></td><td></td><td></td><td></td><td></td></tr>
<tr><td></td><td></td><td></td><td></td><td></td><td></td></tr>
</table>

<table>
<tr><td rowspan="4">ENGLISH</td><td>NAME</td><td>MONDAY</td><td>TUESDAY</td><td>WEDNESDAY</td><td>THURSDAY</td><td>FRIDAY</td></tr>
<tr><td></td><td></td><td></td><td></td><td></td><td></td></tr>
<tr><td></td><td></td><td></td><td></td><td></td><td></td></tr>
<tr><td></td><td></td><td></td><td></td><td></td><td></td></tr>
</table>

<table>
<tr><td>NAME</td><td>MONDAY</td><td>TUESDAY</td><td>WEDNESDAY</td><td>THURSDAY</td><td>FRIDAY</td></tr>
<tr><td></td><td></td><td></td><td></td><td></td><td></td></tr>
<tr><td></td><td></td><td></td><td></td><td></td><td></td></tr>
<tr><td></td><td></td><td></td><td></td><td></td><td></td></tr>
</table>

<table>
<tr><td>NAME</td><td>MONDAY</td><td>TUESDAY</td><td>WEDNESDAY</td><td>THURSDAY</td><td>FRIDAY</td></tr>
<tr><td></td><td></td><td></td><td></td><td></td><td></td></tr>
<tr><td></td><td></td><td></td><td></td><td></td><td></td></tr>
<tr><td></td><td></td><td></td><td></td><td></td><td></td></tr>
</table>

<table>
<tr><td>NAME</td><td>MONDAY</td><td>TUESDAY</td><td>WEDNESDAY</td><td>THURSDAY</td><td>FRIDAY</td></tr>
<tr><td></td><td></td><td></td><td></td><td></td><td></td></tr>
<tr><td></td><td></td><td></td><td></td><td></td><td></td></tr>
<tr><td></td><td></td><td></td><td></td><td></td><td></td></tr>
</table>

<table>
<tr><td>NAME</td><td>MONDAY</td><td>TUESDAY</td><td>WEDNESDAY</td><td>THURSDAY</td><td>FRIDAY</td></tr>
<tr><td></td><td></td><td></td><td></td><td></td><td></td></tr>
<tr><td></td><td></td><td></td><td></td><td></td><td></td></tr>
<tr><td></td><td></td><td></td><td></td><td></td><td></td></tr>
</table>

Weekly ASSIGNMENTS

Week of _____

Name:	○	○
	○	○
	○	○
	○	○

Name:	○	○
	○	○
	○	○
	○	○

Name:	○	○
	○	○
	○	○
	○	○

Videos WATCHED

Name:

Name:

Name:

Brainstorm

Weekly Plan

Week of _____

TO DO'S/*Notes*

_____
_____
_____
_____
_____
_____
_____
_____
_____
_____

_____
_____
_____
_____
_____
_____
_____
_____
_____
_____

Goals

Projects

46

Weekly Curriculum Plan

Week of _____

	NAME	MONDAY	TUESDAY	WEDNESDAY	THURSDAY	FRIDAY
MATH						

	NAME	MONDAY	TUESDAY	WEDNESDAY	THURSDAY	FRIDAY
SCIENCE						

	NAME	MONDAY	TUESDAY	WEDNESDAY	THURSDAY	FRIDAY
HISTORY						

	NAME	MONDAY	TUESDAY	WEDNESDAY	THURSDAY	FRIDAY
ENGLISH						

NAME	MONDAY	TUESDAY	WEDNESDAY	THURSDAY	FRIDAY

NAME	MONDAY	TUESDAY	WEDNESDAY	THURSDAY	FRIDAY

NAME	MONDAY	TUESDAY	WEDNESDAY	THURSDAY	FRIDAY

NAME	MONDAY	TUESDAY	WEDNESDAY	THURSDAY	FRIDAY

Weekly ASSIGNMENTS

Week of _____

Name:	○	○
	○	○
	○	○
	○	○

Name:	○	○
	○	○
	○	○
	○	○

Name:	○	○
	○	○
	○	○
	○	○

Videos WATCHED

Name:

Name:

Name:

Brainstorm

Monthly Reading Register

STUDENT:

Book Title & Author:

○ _____

○ _____

○ _____

STUDENT:

Book Title & Author:

○ _____

○ _____

○ _____

STUDENT:

Book Title & Author:

○ _____

○ _____

○ _____

Monthly Recap & Notes

MONTH   YEAR

SUNDAY	MONDAY	TUESDAY	WEDNESDAY

It takes a BIG HEART to teach little minds

THURSDAY	FRIDAY	SATURDAY	REMINDERS/NOTES
			○ _____ _____ _____ _____
			○ _____ _____ _____
			○ _____ _____ _____
			○ _____ _____ _____
			○ _____ _____ _____ ○ _____ _____ _____ _____

Weekly Plan

Week of _____

TO DO'S/*Notes*

_____
_____
_____
_____
_____
_____
_____
_____
_____
_____
_____

_____
_____
_____
_____
_____
_____
_____
_____
_____
_____
_____
_____

Goals

Projects

Weekly Curriculum Plan

Week of _____

MATH	NAME	MONDAY	TUESDAY	WEDNESDAY	THURSDAY	FRIDAY

SCIENCE	NAME	MONDAY	TUESDAY	WEDNESDAY	THURSDAY	FRIDAY

HISTORY	NAME	MONDAY	TUESDAY	WEDNESDAY	THURSDAY	FRIDAY

ENGLISH	NAME	MONDAY	TUESDAY	WEDNESDAY	THURSDAY	FRIDAY

NAME	MONDAY	TUESDAY	WEDNESDAY	THURSDAY	FRIDAY

NAME	MONDAY	TUESDAY	WEDNESDAY	THURSDAY	FRIDAY

NAME	MONDAY	TUESDAY	WEDNESDAY	THURSDAY	FRIDAY

NAME	MONDAY	TUESDAY	WEDNESDAY	THURSDAY	FRIDAY

Weekly ASSIGNMENTS

Week of _____

Name:	○	○
	○	○
	○	○
	○	○

Name:	○	○
	○	○
	○	○
	○	○

Name:	○	○
	○	○
	○	○
	○	○

Videos WATCHED

Name:

Name:

Name:

Brainstorm

Weekly Plan

Week of _____

TO DO'S/*Notes*

_____
_____
_____
_____
_____
_____
_____
_____
_____
_____
_____

_____
_____
_____
_____
_____
_____
_____
_____
_____
_____
_____

Goals

Projects

Weekly Curriculum Plan

Week of _____

<table>
<tr><td rowspan="4">MATH</td><td>NAME</td><td>MONDAY</td><td>TUESDAY</td><td>WEDNESDAY</td><td>THURSDAY</td><td>FRIDAY</td></tr>
<tr><td></td><td></td><td></td><td></td><td></td><td></td></tr>
<tr><td></td><td></td><td></td><td></td><td></td><td></td></tr>
<tr><td></td><td></td><td></td><td></td><td></td><td></td></tr>
</table>

<table>
<tr><td rowspan="4">SCIENCE</td><td>NAME</td><td>MONDAY</td><td>TUESDAY</td><td>WEDNESDAY</td><td>THURSDAY</td><td>FRIDAY</td></tr>
<tr><td></td><td></td><td></td><td></td><td></td><td></td></tr>
<tr><td></td><td></td><td></td><td></td><td></td><td></td></tr>
<tr><td></td><td></td><td></td><td></td><td></td><td></td></tr>
</table>

<table>
<tr><td rowspan="4">HISTORY</td><td>NAME</td><td>MONDAY</td><td>TUESDAY</td><td>WEDNESDAY</td><td>THURSDAY</td><td>FRIDAY</td></tr>
<tr><td></td><td></td><td></td><td></td><td></td><td></td></tr>
<tr><td></td><td></td><td></td><td></td><td></td><td></td></tr>
<tr><td></td><td></td><td></td><td></td><td></td><td></td></tr>
</table>

<table>
<tr><td rowspan="4">ENGLISH</td><td>NAME</td><td>MONDAY</td><td>TUESDAY</td><td>WEDNESDAY</td><td>THURSDAY</td><td>FRIDAY</td></tr>
<tr><td></td><td></td><td></td><td></td><td></td><td></td></tr>
<tr><td></td><td></td><td></td><td></td><td></td><td></td></tr>
<tr><td></td><td></td><td></td><td></td><td></td><td></td></tr>
</table>

<table>
<tr><td>NAME</td><td>MONDAY</td><td>TUESDAY</td><td>WEDNESDAY</td><td>THURSDAY</td><td>FRIDAY</td></tr>
<tr><td></td><td></td><td></td><td></td><td></td><td></td></tr>
<tr><td></td><td></td><td></td><td></td><td></td><td></td></tr>
<tr><td></td><td></td><td></td><td></td><td></td><td></td></tr>
</table>

<table>
<tr><td>NAME</td><td>MONDAY</td><td>TUESDAY</td><td>WEDNESDAY</td><td>THURSDAY</td><td>FRIDAY</td></tr>
<tr><td></td><td></td><td></td><td></td><td></td><td></td></tr>
<tr><td></td><td></td><td></td><td></td><td></td><td></td></tr>
<tr><td></td><td></td><td></td><td></td><td></td><td></td></tr>
</table>

<table>
<tr><td>NAME</td><td>MONDAY</td><td>TUESDAY</td><td>WEDNESDAY</td><td>THURSDAY</td><td>FRIDAY</td></tr>
<tr><td></td><td></td><td></td><td></td><td></td><td></td></tr>
<tr><td></td><td></td><td></td><td></td><td></td><td></td></tr>
<tr><td></td><td></td><td></td><td></td><td></td><td></td></tr>
</table>

<table>
<tr><td>NAME</td><td>MONDAY</td><td>TUESDAY</td><td>WEDNESDAY</td><td>THURSDAY</td><td>FRIDAY</td></tr>
<tr><td></td><td></td><td></td><td></td><td></td><td></td></tr>
<tr><td></td><td></td><td></td><td></td><td></td><td></td></tr>
<tr><td></td><td></td><td></td><td></td><td></td><td></td></tr>
</table>

Weekly ASSIGNMENTS

Week of _____

Name:	○	○
	○	○
	○	○
	○	○

Name:	○	○
	○	○
	○	○
	○	○

Name:	○	○
	○	○
	○	○
	○	○

Videos WATCHED

Name:

Name:

Name:

Brainstorm

Weekly Plan

Week of _____

TO DO'S/*Notes*

_____
_____
_____
_____
_____
_____
_____
_____
_____
_____
_____

_____
_____
_____
_____
_____
_____
_____
_____
_____
_____
_____

Goals

Projects

Weekly Curriculum Plan

Week of _____

	NAME	MONDAY	TUESDAY	WEDNESDAY	THURSDAY	FRIDAY
MATH						

	NAME	MONDAY	TUESDAY	WEDNESDAY	THURSDAY	FRIDAY
SCIENCE						

	NAME	MONDAY	TUESDAY	WEDNESDAY	THURSDAY	FRIDAY
HISTORY						

	NAME	MONDAY	TUESDAY	WEDNESDAY	THURSDAY	FRIDAY
ENGLISH						

NAME	MONDAY	TUESDAY	WEDNESDAY	THURSDAY	FRIDAY

NAME	MONDAY	TUESDAY	WEDNESDAY	THURSDAY	FRIDAY

NAME	MONDAY	TUESDAY	WEDNESDAY	THURSDAY	FRIDAY

NAME	MONDAY	TUESDAY	WEDNESDAY	THURSDAY	FRIDAY

Weekly ASSIGNMENTS

Week of _____

Name:	○	○
	○	○
	○	○
	○	○

Name:	○	○
	○	○
	○	○
	○	○

Name:	○	○
	○	○
	○	○
	○	○

Videos WATCHED

Name:

Name:

Name:

Brainstorm

Weekly Plan

Week of _____

TO DO'S/*Notes*

_____
_____
_____
_____
_____
_____
_____
_____
_____
_____
_____

_____
_____
_____
_____
_____
_____
_____
_____
_____
_____
_____

Goals

Projects

Weekly Curriculum Plan

Week of _____

MATH

NAME	MONDAY	TUESDAY	WEDNESDAY	THURSDAY	FRIDAY

SCIENCE

NAME	MONDAY	TUESDAY	WEDNESDAY	THURSDAY	FRIDAY

HISTORY

NAME	MONDAY	TUESDAY	WEDNESDAY	THURSDAY	FRIDAY

ENGLISH

NAME	MONDAY	TUESDAY	WEDNESDAY	THURSDAY	FRIDAY

NAME	MONDAY	TUESDAY	WEDNESDAY	THURSDAY	FRIDAY

NAME	MONDAY	TUESDAY	WEDNESDAY	THURSDAY	FRIDAY

NAME	MONDAY	TUESDAY	WEDNESDAY	THURSDAY	FRIDAY

NAME	MONDAY	TUESDAY	WEDNESDAY	THURSDAY	FRIDAY

Weekly ASSIGNMENTS

Week of _____

Name:	○	○
	○	○
	○	○
	○	○

Name:	○	○
	○	○
	○	○
	○	○

Name:	○	○
	○	○
	○	○
	○	○

Videos WATCHED

Name:

Name:

Name:

Brainstorm

Monthly Reading Register

STUDENT:

Book Title & Author:

○ _____

○ _____

○ _____

STUDENT:

Book Title & Author:

○ _____

○ _____

○ _____

STUDENT:

Book Title & Author:

○ _____

○ _____

○ _____

Monthly Recap & Notes

MONTH   YEAR

SUNDAY	MONDAY	TUESDAY	WEDNESDAY

It takes a BIG HEART to teach little minds

THURSDAY	FRIDAY	SATURDAY	REMINDERS/NOTES
			○ _____ _____ _____ _____
			○ _____ _____ _____ _____
			○ _____ _____ _____
			○ _____ _____ _____ _____
			○ _____ _____ ○ _____ _____ _____

73

Weekly Plan

Week of _____

TO DO'S/*Notes*

_____
_____
_____
_____
_____
_____
_____
_____
_____
_____
_____

_____
_____
_____
_____
_____
_____
_____
_____
_____
_____
_____

Goals

Projects

Weekly Curriculum Plan

Week of _____

MATH

NAME	MONDAY	TUESDAY	WEDNESDAY	THURSDAY	FRIDAY

SCIENCE

NAME	MONDAY	TUESDAY	WEDNESDAY	THURSDAY	FRIDAY

HISTORY

NAME	MONDAY	TUESDAY	WEDNESDAY	THURSDAY	FRIDAY

ENGLISH

NAME	MONDAY	TUESDAY	WEDNESDAY	THURSDAY	FRIDAY

NAME	MONDAY	TUESDAY	WEDNESDAY	THURSDAY	FRIDAY

NAME	MONDAY	TUESDAY	WEDNESDAY	THURSDAY	FRIDAY

NAME	MONDAY	TUESDAY	WEDNESDAY	THURSDAY	FRIDAY

NAME	MONDAY	TUESDAY	WEDNESDAY	THURSDAY	FRIDAY

Weekly ASSIGNMENTS

Week of _____

Name:	○	○
	○	○
	○	○
	○	○

Name:	○	○
	○	○
	○	○
	○	○

Name:	○	○
	○	○
	○	○
	○	○

Videos WATCHED

Name:

Name:

Name:

Brainstorm

Weekly Plan

Week of _____

TO DO'S/*Notes*

_____
_____
_____
_____
_____
_____
_____
_____
_____
_____

_____
_____
_____
_____
_____
_____
_____
_____
_____
_____

Goals

Projects

Weekly Curriculum Plan

Week of _____

MATH	NAME	MONDAY	TUESDAY	WEDNESDAY	THURSDAY	FRIDAY

SCIENCE	NAME	MONDAY	TUESDAY	WEDNESDAY	THURSDAY	FRIDAY

HISTORY	NAME	MONDAY	TUESDAY	WEDNESDAY	THURSDAY	FRIDAY

ENGLISH	NAME	MONDAY	TUESDAY	WEDNESDAY	THURSDAY	FRIDAY

NAME	MONDAY	TUESDAY	WEDNESDAY	THURSDAY	FRIDAY

NAME	MONDAY	TUESDAY	WEDNESDAY	THURSDAY	FRIDAY

NAME	MONDAY	TUESDAY	WEDNESDAY	THURSDAY	FRIDAY

NAME	MONDAY	TUESDAY	WEDNESDAY	THURSDAY	FRIDAY

Weekly ASSIGNMENTS

Week of _____

Name:	○		○	
	○		○	
	○		○	
	○		○	

Name:	○		○	
	○		○	
	○		○	
	○		○	

Name:	○		○	
	○		○	
	○		○	
	○		○	

Videos WATCHED

Name:

Name:

Name:

Brainstorm

Weekly Plan

Week of _____

TO DO'S/*Notes*

_____
_____
_____
_____
_____
_____
_____
_____
_____
_____

_____
_____
_____
_____
_____
_____
_____
_____
_____
_____

Goals

Projects

Weekly Curriculum Plan

Week of _____

	NAME	MONDAY	TUESDAY	WEDNESDAY	THURSDAY	FRIDAY
MATH						

	NAME	MONDAY	TUESDAY	WEDNESDAY	THURSDAY	FRIDAY
SCIENCE						

	NAME	MONDAY	TUESDAY	WEDNESDAY	THURSDAY	FRIDAY
HISTORY						

	NAME	MONDAY	TUESDAY	WEDNESDAY	THURSDAY	FRIDAY
ENGLISH						

NAME	MONDAY	TUESDAY	WEDNESDAY	THURSDAY	FRIDAY

NAME	MONDAY	TUESDAY	WEDNESDAY	THURSDAY	FRIDAY

NAME	MONDAY	TUESDAY	WEDNESDAY	THURSDAY	FRIDAY

NAME	MONDAY	TUESDAY	WEDNESDAY	THURSDAY	FRIDAY

Weekly ASSIGNMENTS

Week of _____

Name:	○	○
	○	○
	○	○
	○	○

Name:	○	○
	○	○
	○	○
	○	○

Name:	○	○
	○	○
	○	○
	○	○

Videos WATCHED

Name:

Name:

Name:

Brainstorm

Weekly Plan

Week of _____

_____

_____

_____

_____

_____

_____

_____

_____

_____

_____

_____

_____

_____

_____

_____

_____

_____

_____

_____

_____

_____

_____

_____

Goals

Projects

Weekly Curriculum Plan

Week of _____

MATH

NAME	MONDAY	TUESDAY	WEDNESDAY	THURSDAY	FRIDAY

SCIENCE

NAME	MONDAY	TUESDAY	WEDNESDAY	THURSDAY	FRIDAY

HISTORY

NAME	MONDAY	TUESDAY	WEDNESDAY	THURSDAY	FRIDAY

ENGLISH

NAME	MONDAY	TUESDAY	WEDNESDAY	THURSDAY	FRIDAY

NAME	MONDAY	TUESDAY	WEDNESDAY	THURSDAY	FRIDAY

NAME	MONDAY	TUESDAY	WEDNESDAY	THURSDAY	FRIDAY

NAME	MONDAY	TUESDAY	WEDNESDAY	THURSDAY	FRIDAY

NAME	MONDAY	TUESDAY	WEDNESDAY	THURSDAY	FRIDAY

Weekly ASSIGNMENTS

Week of _____

Name:	○		○	
	○		○	
	○		○	
	○		○	

Name:	○		○	
	○		○	
	○		○	
	○		○	

Name:	○		○	
	○		○	
	○		○	
	○		○	

Videos WATCHED

Name:

Name:

Name:

Brainstorm

Monthly Reading Register

STUDENT:

Book Title & Author:

○ _____

○ _____

○ _____

STUDENT:

Book Title & Author:

○ _____

○ _____

○ _____

STUDENT:

Book Title & Author:

○ _____

○ _____

○ _____

Monthly Recap & Notes

MONTH _____   YEAR _____

SUNDAY	MONDAY	TUESDAY	WEDNESDAY

It takes a BIG HEART to teach little minds

THURSDAY	FRIDAY	SATURDAY	REMINDERS/NOTES
			○ _____ _____ _____ _____ _____
			○ _____ _____ _____ _____ _____
			○ _____ _____ _____ _____ _____
			○ _____ _____ _____ _____ _____
			○ _____ ○ _____ _____ _____ _____

Weekly Plan

Week of _____

TO DO'S/*Notes*

_____
_____
_____
_____
_____
_____
_____
_____
_____
_____
_____

_____
_____
_____
_____
_____
_____
_____
_____
_____
_____
_____

Goals

Projects

Weekly Curriculum Plan

Week of _____

	NAME	MONDAY	TUESDAY	WEDNESDAY	THURSDAY	FRIDAY
MATH						

	NAME	MONDAY	TUESDAY	WEDNESDAY	THURSDAY	FRIDAY
SCIENCE						

	NAME	MONDAY	TUESDAY	WEDNESDAY	THURSDAY	FRIDAY
HISTORY						

	NAME	MONDAY	TUESDAY	WEDNESDAY	THURSDAY	FRIDAY
ENGLISH						

NAME	MONDAY	TUESDAY	WEDNESDAY	THURSDAY	FRIDAY

NAME	MONDAY	TUESDAY	WEDNESDAY	THURSDAY	FRIDAY

NAME	MONDAY	TUESDAY	WEDNESDAY	THURSDAY	FRIDAY

NAME	MONDAY	TUESDAY	WEDNESDAY	THURSDAY	FRIDAY

Weekly ASSIGNMENTS

Week of _____

Name:	○		○	
	○		○	
	○		○	
	○		○	

Name:	○		○	
	○		○	
	○		○	
	○		○	

Name:	○		○	
	○		○	
	○		○	
	○		○	

Videos WATCHED

Name:

Name:

Name:

Brainstorm

Weekly Plan

Week of _____

TO DO'S/*Notes*

_____
_____
_____
_____
_____
_____
_____
_____
_____
_____

_____
_____
_____
_____
_____
_____
_____
_____
_____
_____
_____

Goals

Projects

Weekly Curriculum Plan

Week of _____

MATH

NAME	MONDAY	TUESDAY	WEDNESDAY	THURSDAY	FRIDAY

SCIENCE

NAME	MONDAY	TUESDAY	WEDNESDAY	THURSDAY	FRIDAY

HISTORY

NAME	MONDAY	TUESDAY	WEDNESDAY	THURSDAY	FRIDAY

ENGLISH

NAME	MONDAY	TUESDAY	WEDNESDAY	THURSDAY	FRIDAY

NAME	MONDAY	TUESDAY	WEDNESDAY	THURSDAY	FRIDAY

NAME	MONDAY	TUESDAY	WEDNESDAY	THURSDAY	FRIDAY

NAME	MONDAY	TUESDAY	WEDNESDAY	THURSDAY	FRIDAY

NAME	MONDAY	TUESDAY	WEDNESDAY	THURSDAY	FRIDAY

Weekly ASSIGNMENTS

Week of _____

Name:	○		○	
	○		○	
	○		○	
	○		○	

Name:	○		○	
	○		○	
	○		○	
	○		○	

Name:	○		○	
	○		○	
	○		○	
	○		○	

Videos WATCHED

Name:

Name:

Name:

Brainstorm

Weekly Plan

Week of _____

TO DO'S/*Notes*

_____
_____
_____
_____
_____
_____
_____
_____
_____
_____

_____
_____
_____
_____
_____
_____
_____
_____
_____
_____

Goals

Projects

Weekly Curriculum Plan

Week of _____

MATH

NAME	MONDAY	TUESDAY	WEDNESDAY	THURSDAY	FRIDAY

SCIENCE

NAME	MONDAY	TUESDAY	WEDNESDAY	THURSDAY	FRIDAY

HISTORY

NAME	MONDAY	TUESDAY	WEDNESDAY	THURSDAY	FRIDAY

ENGLISH

NAME	MONDAY	TUESDAY	WEDNESDAY	THURSDAY	FRIDAY

NAME	MONDAY	TUESDAY	WEDNESDAY	THURSDAY	FRIDAY

NAME	MONDAY	TUESDAY	WEDNESDAY	THURSDAY	FRIDAY

NAME	MONDAY	TUESDAY	WEDNESDAY	THURSDAY	FRIDAY

NAME	MONDAY	TUESDAY	WEDNESDAY	THURSDAY	FRIDAY

Weekly ASSIGNMENTS

Week of _____

Name:	○		○	
	○		○	
	○		○	
	○		○	

Name:	○		○	
	○		○	
	○		○	
	○		○	

Name:	○		○	
	○		○	
	○		○	
	○		○	

Videos WATCHED

Name:

Name:

Name:

Brainstorm

Weekly Plan

Week of _____

TO DO'S/*Notes*

_____
_____
_____
_____
_____
_____
_____
_____
_____
_____

_____
_____
_____
_____
_____
_____
_____
_____
_____
_____

Goals

Projects

Weekly Curriculum Plan

Week of _____

<table>
<tr><th></th><th>NAME</th><th>MONDAY</th><th>TUESDAY</th><th>WEDNESDAY</th><th>THURSDAY</th><th>FRIDAY</th></tr>
<tr><td rowspan="3">MATH</td><td></td><td></td><td></td><td></td><td></td><td></td></tr>
<tr><td></td><td></td><td></td><td></td><td></td><td></td></tr>
<tr><td></td><td></td><td></td><td></td><td></td><td></td></tr>
</table>

<table>
<tr><th></th><th>NAME</th><th>MONDAY</th><th>TUESDAY</th><th>WEDNESDAY</th><th>THURSDAY</th><th>FRIDAY</th></tr>
<tr><td rowspan="3">SCIENCE</td><td></td><td></td><td></td><td></td><td></td><td></td></tr>
<tr><td></td><td></td><td></td><td></td><td></td><td></td></tr>
<tr><td></td><td></td><td></td><td></td><td></td><td></td></tr>
</table>

<table>
<tr><th></th><th>NAME</th><th>MONDAY</th><th>TUESDAY</th><th>WEDNESDAY</th><th>THURSDAY</th><th>FRIDAY</th></tr>
<tr><td rowspan="3">HISTORY</td><td></td><td></td><td></td><td></td><td></td><td></td></tr>
<tr><td></td><td></td><td></td><td></td><td></td><td></td></tr>
<tr><td></td><td></td><td></td><td></td><td></td><td></td></tr>
</table>

<table>
<tr><th></th><th>NAME</th><th>MONDAY</th><th>TUESDAY</th><th>WEDNESDAY</th><th>THURSDAY</th><th>FRIDAY</th></tr>
<tr><td rowspan="3">ENGLISH</td><td></td><td></td><td></td><td></td><td></td><td></td></tr>
<tr><td></td><td></td><td></td><td></td><td></td><td></td></tr>
<tr><td></td><td></td><td></td><td></td><td></td><td></td></tr>
</table>

<table>
<tr><th>NAME</th><th>MONDAY</th><th>TUESDAY</th><th>WEDNESDAY</th><th>THURSDAY</th><th>FRIDAY</th></tr>
<tr><td></td><td></td><td></td><td></td><td></td><td></td></tr>
<tr><td></td><td></td><td></td><td></td><td></td><td></td></tr>
<tr><td></td><td></td><td></td><td></td><td></td><td></td></tr>
</table>

<table>
<tr><th>NAME</th><th>MONDAY</th><th>TUESDAY</th><th>WEDNESDAY</th><th>THURSDAY</th><th>FRIDAY</th></tr>
<tr><td></td><td></td><td></td><td></td><td></td><td></td></tr>
<tr><td></td><td></td><td></td><td></td><td></td><td></td></tr>
<tr><td></td><td></td><td></td><td></td><td></td><td></td></tr>
</table>

<table>
<tr><th>NAME</th><th>MONDAY</th><th>TUESDAY</th><th>WEDNESDAY</th><th>THURSDAY</th><th>FRIDAY</th></tr>
<tr><td></td><td></td><td></td><td></td><td></td><td></td></tr>
<tr><td></td><td></td><td></td><td></td><td></td><td></td></tr>
<tr><td></td><td></td><td></td><td></td><td></td><td></td></tr>
</table>

<table>
<tr><th>NAME</th><th>MONDAY</th><th>TUESDAY</th><th>WEDNESDAY</th><th>THURSDAY</th><th>FRIDAY</th></tr>
<tr><td></td><td></td><td></td><td></td><td></td><td></td></tr>
<tr><td></td><td></td><td></td><td></td><td></td><td></td></tr>
<tr><td></td><td></td><td></td><td></td><td></td><td></td></tr>
</table>

Weekly ASSIGNMENTS

Week of _____

Name:	○	○
	○	○
	○	○
	○	○

Name:	○	○
	○	○
	○	○
	○	○

Name:	○	○
	○	○
	○	○
	○	○

Videos WATCHED

Name:

Name:

Name:

Brainstorm

Monthly Reading Register

STUDENT:

Book Title & Author:

○ _____

○ _____

○ _____

STUDENT:

Book Title & Author:

○ _____

○ _____

○ _____

STUDENT:

Book Title & Author:

○ _____

○ _____

○ _____

Monthly Recap & Notes

_____

_____

_____

_____

_____

_____

_____

_____

_____

_____

_____

_____

_____

_____

_____

MONTH   YEAR

SUNDAY	MONDAY	TUESDAY	WEDNESDAY

MONTH   YEAR

It takes a BIG HEART to teach little minds

THURSDAY	FRIDAY	SATURDAY	REMINDERS/NOTES
			○ _____ _____ _____ _____
			○ _____ _____ _____ _____
			○ _____ _____ _____ _____
			○ _____ _____ _____ _____
			○ _____ _____ _____ ○ _____ _____ _____ _____

Weekly Plan

Week of _____

TO DO'S/*Notes*

_____
_____
_____
_____
_____
_____
_____
_____
_____
_____

_____
_____
_____
_____
_____
_____
_____
_____
_____
_____

Goals

Projects

Weekly Curriculum Plan

Week of _____

MATH

NAME	MONDAY	TUESDAY	WEDNESDAY	THURSDAY	FRIDAY

SCIENCE

NAME	MONDAY	TUESDAY	WEDNESDAY	THURSDAY	FRIDAY

HISTORY

NAME	MONDAY	TUESDAY	WEDNESDAY	THURSDAY	FRIDAY

ENGLISH

NAME	MONDAY	TUESDAY	WEDNESDAY	THURSDAY	FRIDAY

NAME	MONDAY	TUESDAY	WEDNESDAY	THURSDAY	FRIDAY

NAME	MONDAY	TUESDAY	WEDNESDAY	THURSDAY	FRIDAY

NAME	MONDAY	TUESDAY	WEDNESDAY	THURSDAY	FRIDAY

NAME	MONDAY	TUESDAY	WEDNESDAY	THURSDAY	FRIDAY

Weekly ASSIGNMENTS

Week of _____

Name:	○	○
	○	○
	○	○
	○	○

Name:	○	○
	○	○
	○	○
	○	○

Name:	○	○
	○	○
	○	○
	○	○

Videos WATCHED

Name:

Name:

Name:

Brainstorm

Weekly Plan

Week of _____

TO DO'S/Notes

_____
_____
_____
_____
_____
_____
_____
_____
_____
_____
_____

_____
_____
_____
_____
_____
_____
_____
_____
_____
_____
_____

Goals

Projects

Weekly Curriculum Plan

Week of _____

MATH

NAME	MONDAY	TUESDAY	WEDNESDAY	THURSDAY	FRIDAY

SCIENCE

NAME	MONDAY	TUESDAY	WEDNESDAY	THURSDAY	FRIDAY

HISTORY

NAME	MONDAY	TUESDAY	WEDNESDAY	THURSDAY	FRIDAY

ENGLISH

NAME	MONDAY	TUESDAY	WEDNESDAY	THURSDAY	FRIDAY

NAME	MONDAY	TUESDAY	WEDNESDAY	THURSDAY	FRIDAY

NAME	MONDAY	TUESDAY	WEDNESDAY	THURSDAY	FRIDAY

NAME	MONDAY	TUESDAY	WEDNESDAY	THURSDAY	FRIDAY

NAME	MONDAY	TUESDAY	WEDNESDAY	THURSDAY	FRIDAY

Weekly ASSIGNMENTS

Week of _____

Name:	○	○
	○	○
	○	○
	○	○

Name:	○	○
	○	○
	○	○
	○	○

Name:	○	○
	○	○
	○	○
	○	○

Videos WATCHED

Name:

Name:

Name:

Brainstorm

Weekly Plan

Week of _____

TO DO'S/Notes

_____
_____
_____
_____
_____
_____
_____
_____
_____
_____

_____
_____
_____
_____
_____
_____
_____
_____
_____
_____

Goals

Projects

Weekly Curriculum Plan

Week of _____

<table>
<tr><td rowspan="4">MATH</td><td>NAME</td><td>MONDAY</td><td>TUESDAY</td><td>WEDNESDAY</td><td>THURSDAY</td><td>FRIDAY</td></tr>
<tr><td></td><td></td><td></td><td></td><td></td><td></td></tr>
<tr><td></td><td></td><td></td><td></td><td></td><td></td></tr>
<tr><td></td><td></td><td></td><td></td><td></td><td></td></tr>
</table>

<table>
<tr><td rowspan="4">SCIENCE</td><td>NAME</td><td>MONDAY</td><td>TUESDAY</td><td>WEDNESDAY</td><td>THURSDAY</td><td>FRIDAY</td></tr>
<tr><td></td><td></td><td></td><td></td><td></td><td></td></tr>
<tr><td></td><td></td><td></td><td></td><td></td><td></td></tr>
<tr><td></td><td></td><td></td><td></td><td></td><td></td></tr>
</table>

<table>
<tr><td rowspan="4">HISTORY</td><td>NAME</td><td>MONDAY</td><td>TUESDAY</td><td>WEDNESDAY</td><td>THURSDAY</td><td>FRIDAY</td></tr>
<tr><td></td><td></td><td></td><td></td><td></td><td></td></tr>
<tr><td></td><td></td><td></td><td></td><td></td><td></td></tr>
<tr><td></td><td></td><td></td><td></td><td></td><td></td></tr>
</table>

<table>
<tr><td rowspan="4">ENGLISH</td><td>NAME</td><td>MONDAY</td><td>TUESDAY</td><td>WEDNESDAY</td><td>THURSDAY</td><td>FRIDAY</td></tr>
<tr><td></td><td></td><td></td><td></td><td></td><td></td></tr>
<tr><td></td><td></td><td></td><td></td><td></td><td></td></tr>
<tr><td></td><td></td><td></td><td></td><td></td><td></td></tr>
</table>

<table>
<tr><td>NAME</td><td>MONDAY</td><td>TUESDAY</td><td>WEDNESDAY</td><td>THURSDAY</td><td>FRIDAY</td></tr>
<tr><td></td><td></td><td></td><td></td><td></td><td></td></tr>
<tr><td></td><td></td><td></td><td></td><td></td><td></td></tr>
<tr><td></td><td></td><td></td><td></td><td></td><td></td></tr>
</table>

<table>
<tr><td>NAME</td><td>MONDAY</td><td>TUESDAY</td><td>WEDNESDAY</td><td>THURSDAY</td><td>FRIDAY</td></tr>
<tr><td></td><td></td><td></td><td></td><td></td><td></td></tr>
<tr><td></td><td></td><td></td><td></td><td></td><td></td></tr>
<tr><td></td><td></td><td></td><td></td><td></td><td></td></tr>
</table>

<table>
<tr><td>NAME</td><td>MONDAY</td><td>TUESDAY</td><td>WEDNESDAY</td><td>THURSDAY</td><td>FRIDAY</td></tr>
<tr><td></td><td></td><td></td><td></td><td></td><td></td></tr>
<tr><td></td><td></td><td></td><td></td><td></td><td></td></tr>
<tr><td></td><td></td><td></td><td></td><td></td><td></td></tr>
</table>

<table>
<tr><td>NAME</td><td>MONDAY</td><td>TUESDAY</td><td>WEDNESDAY</td><td>THURSDAY</td><td>FRIDAY</td></tr>
<tr><td></td><td></td><td></td><td></td><td></td><td></td></tr>
<tr><td></td><td></td><td></td><td></td><td></td><td></td></tr>
<tr><td></td><td></td><td></td><td></td><td></td><td></td></tr>
</table>

Weekly ASSIGNMENTS

Week of _____

Name:	○	○
	○	○
	○	○
	○	○

Name:	○	○
	○	○
	○	○
	○	○

Name:	○	○
	○	○
	○	○
	○	○

Videos WATCHED

Name:

Name:

Name:

Brainstorm

Weekly Plan

Week of _____

TO DO'S/*Notes*

_____
_____
_____
_____
_____
_____
_____
_____
_____
_____

_____
_____
_____
_____
_____
_____
_____
_____
_____
_____

Goals

Projects

Weekly Curriculum Plan

Week of _____

<table>
<tr><td rowspan="2">MATH</td><td>NAME</td><td>MONDAY</td><td>TUESDAY</td><td>WEDNESDAY</td><td>THURSDAY</td><td>FRIDAY</td></tr>
<tr><td></td><td></td><td></td><td></td><td></td><td></td></tr>
</table>

MATH	NAME	MONDAY	TUESDAY	WEDNESDAY	THURSDAY	FRIDAY

SCIENCE	NAME	MONDAY	TUESDAY	WEDNESDAY	THURSDAY	FRIDAY

HISTORY	NAME	MONDAY	TUESDAY	WEDNESDAY	THURSDAY	FRIDAY

ENGLISH	NAME	MONDAY	TUESDAY	WEDNESDAY	THURSDAY	FRIDAY

	NAME	MONDAY	TUESDAY	WEDNESDAY	THURSDAY	FRIDAY

	NAME	MONDAY	TUESDAY	WEDNESDAY	THURSDAY	FRIDAY

	NAME	MONDAY	TUESDAY	WEDNESDAY	THURSDAY	FRIDAY

	NAME	MONDAY	TUESDAY	WEDNESDAY	THURSDAY	FRIDAY

Weekly ASSIGNMENTS

Week of _____

Name:	○	○
	○	○
	○	○
	○	○

Name:	○	○
	○	○
	○	○
	○	○

Name:	○	○
	○	○
	○	○
	○	○

Videos WATCHED

Name:

Name:

Name:

Brainstorm

Monthly Reading Register

STUDENT:

Book Title & Author:

○ _____

○ _____

○ _____

STUDENT:

Book Title & Author:

○ _____

○ _____

○ _____

STUDENT:

Book Title & Author:

○ _____

○ _____

○ _____

Monthly Recap & Notes

ATTENDANCE REGISTER | Semester 1

Name: _____

	July	August	September	October	November	December
1						
2						
3						
4						
5						
6						
7						
8						
9						
10						
11						
12						
13						
14						
15						
16						
17						
18						
19						
20						
21						
22						
23						
24						
25						
26						
27						
28						
29						
30						
31						

GRADE REGISTER | *Semester 1*

Name: _____

Subject: _____   Subject: _____

Date	Assignment	Points Possible	Points Achieved	Grade
Semester 1 Grade				

Date	Assignment	Points Possible	Points Achieved	Grade
Semester 1 Grade				

GRADE REGISTER | Semester 1

Name: _____

Subject: _____

Date	Assignment	Points Possible	Points Achieved	Grade
Semester 1 Grade				

Subject: _____

Date	Assignment	Points Possible	Points Achieved	Grade
Semester 1 Grade				

GRADE REGISTER | *Semester 1*

Name: _____

Subject: _____

Date	Assignment	Points Possible	Points Achieved	Grade
Semester 1 Grade				

Subject: _____

Date	Assignment	Points Possible	Points Achieved	Grade
Semester 1 Grade				

GRADE REGISTER | *Semester 1*

Name: _____

Subject: _____   Subject: _____

Date	Assignment	Points Possible	Points Achieved	Grade
Semester 1 Grade				

Date	Assignment	Points Possible	Points Achieved	Grade
Semester 1 Grade				

ATTENDANCE REGISTER | *Semester 1*

Name: _____

	July	August	September	October	November	December
1						
2						
3						
4						
5						
6						
7						
8						
9						
10						
11						
12						
13						
14						
15						
16						
17						
18						
19						
20						
21						
22						
23						
24						
25						
26						
27						
28						
29						
30						
31						

GRADE REGISTER | Semester 1

Name: _____

Subject: _____

Date	Assignment	Points Possible	Points Achieved	Grade
Semester 1 Grade				

Subject: _____

Date	Assignment	Points Possible	Points Achieved	Grade
Semester 1 Grade				

GRADE REGISTER | *Semester 1*

Name: _____

Subject: _____

Date	Assignment	Points Possible	Points Achieved	Grade
Semester 1 Grade				

Subject: _____

Date	Assignment	Points Possible	Points Achieved	Grade
Semester 1 Grade				

GRADE REGISTER | *Semester 1*

Name: _____

Subject: _____

Date	Assignment	Points Possible	Points Achieved	Grade
Semester 1 Grade				

Subject: _____

Date	Assignment	Points Possible	Points Achieved	Grade
Semester 1 Grade				

GRADE REGISTER | *Semester 1*

Name: _____

Subject: _____   Subject: _____

Date	Assignment	Points Possible	Points Achieved	Grade
Semester 1 Grade				

Date	Assignment	Points Possible	Points Achieved	Grade
Semester 1 Grade				

ATTENDANCE REGISTER | Semester 1

Name: _____

	July	August	September	October	November	December
1						
2						
3						
4						
5						
6						
7						
8						
9						
10						
11						
12						
13						
14						
15						
16						
17						
18						
19						
20						
21						
22						
23						
24						
25						
26						
27						
28						
29						
30						
31						

GRADE REGISTER | *Semester 1*

Name: _____

Subject: _____

Date	Assignment	Points Possible	Points Achieved	Grade
Semester 1 Grade				

Subject: _____

Date	Assignment	Points Possible	Points Achieved	Grade
Semester 1 Grade				

GRADE REGISTER | *Semester 1*

Name: _____

Subject: _____

Date	Assignment	Points Possible	Points Achieved	Grade
Semester 1 Grade				

Subject: _____

Date	Assignment	Points Possible	Points Achieved	Grade
Semester 1 Grade				

GRADE REGISTER | *Semester 1*

Name: _____

Subject: _____

Date	Assignment	Points Possible	Points Achieved	Grade
Semester 1 Grade				

Subject: _____

Date	Assignment	Points Possible	Points Achieved	Grade
Semester 1 Grade				

GRADE REGISTER | *Semester 1*

Name: _____

Subject: _____

Date	Assignment	Points Possible	Points Achieved	Grade
Semester 1 Grade				

Subject: _____

Date	Assignment	Points Possible	Points Achieved	Grade
Semester 1 Grade				

You DON'T HAVE — TO HAVE IT ALL — Figured Out TO MOVE Forward... JUST TAKE THE NEXT STEP

MONTH

YEAR

SUNDAY	MONDAY	TUESDAY	WEDNESDAY

It takes a BIG HEART to teach little minds

THURSDAY	FRIDAY	SATURDAY	REMINDERS/NOTES
			○ _____ _____ _____ _____
			○ _____ _____ _____ _____
			○ _____ _____ _____ _____
			○ _____ _____ _____ _____
			○ _____ _____ _____

Weekly Plan

Week of _____

TO DO'S/*Notes*

_____
_____
_____
_____
_____
_____
_____
_____
_____
_____

_____
_____
_____
_____
_____
_____
_____
_____
_____
_____

Goals

Projects

Weekly Curriculum Plan

Week of _____

MATH	NAME	MONDAY	TUESDAY	WEDNESDAY	THURSDAY	FRIDAY

SCIENCE	NAME	MONDAY	TUESDAY	WEDNESDAY	THURSDAY	FRIDAY

HISTORY	NAME	MONDAY	TUESDAY	WEDNESDAY	THURSDAY	FRIDAY

ENGLISH	NAME	MONDAY	TUESDAY	WEDNESDAY	THURSDAY	FRIDAY

	NAME	MONDAY	TUESDAY	WEDNESDAY	THURSDAY	FRIDAY

	NAME	MONDAY	TUESDAY	WEDNESDAY	THURSDAY	FRIDAY

	NAME	MONDAY	TUESDAY	WEDNESDAY	THURSDAY	FRIDAY

	NAME	MONDAY	TUESDAY	WEDNESDAY	THURSDAY	FRIDAY

Weekly ASSIGNMENTS

Week of _____

Name:	○		○
	○		○
	○		○
	○		○

Name:	○		○
	○		○
	○		○
	○		○

Name:	○		○
	○		○
	○		○
	○		○

Videos WATCHED

Name:

Name:

Name:

Brainstorm

Weekly Plan

Week of _____

TO DO'S/*Notes*

_____
_____
_____
_____
_____
_____
_____
_____
_____
_____
_____

_____
_____
_____
_____
_____
_____
_____
_____
_____
_____
_____
_____

Goals

Projects

Weekly Curriculum Plan

Week of _____

MATH

NAME	MONDAY	TUESDAY	WEDNESDAY	THURSDAY	FRIDAY

SCIENCE

NAME	MONDAY	TUESDAY	WEDNESDAY	THURSDAY	FRIDAY

HISTORY

NAME	MONDAY	TUESDAY	WEDNESDAY	THURSDAY	FRIDAY

ENGLISH

NAME	MONDAY	TUESDAY	WEDNESDAY	THURSDAY	FRIDAY

NAME	MONDAY	TUESDAY	WEDNESDAY	THURSDAY	FRIDAY

NAME	MONDAY	TUESDAY	WEDNESDAY	THURSDAY	FRIDAY

NAME	MONDAY	TUESDAY	WEDNESDAY	THURSDAY	FRIDAY

NAME	MONDAY	TUESDAY	WEDNESDAY	THURSDAY	FRIDAY

Weekly ASSIGNMENTS

Week of _____

Name:	○		○	
	○		○	
	○		○	
	○		○	

Name:	○		○	
	○		○	
	○		○	
	○		○	

Name:	○		○	
	○		○	
	○		○	
	○		○	

Videos WATCHED

Name:

Name:

Name:

Brainstorm

Weekly Plan

Week of _____

TO DO'S/*Notes*

_____
_____
_____
_____
_____
_____
_____
_____
_____
_____

_____
_____
_____
_____
_____
_____
_____
_____
_____
_____
_____

Goals

Projects

Weekly Curriculum Plan

Week of _____

MATH

NAME	MONDAY	TUESDAY	WEDNESDAY	THURSDAY	FRIDAY

MATH

NAME	MONDAY	TUESDAY	WEDNESDAY	THURSDAY	FRIDAY

SCIENCE

NAME	MONDAY	TUESDAY	WEDNESDAY	THURSDAY	FRIDAY

HISTORY

NAME	MONDAY	TUESDAY	WEDNESDAY	THURSDAY	FRIDAY

ENGLISH

NAME	MONDAY	TUESDAY	WEDNESDAY	THURSDAY	FRIDAY

NAME	MONDAY	TUESDAY	WEDNESDAY	THURSDAY	FRIDAY

NAME	MONDAY	TUESDAY	WEDNESDAY	THURSDAY	FRIDAY

NAME	MONDAY	TUESDAY	WEDNESDAY	THURSDAY	FRIDAY

Weekly ASSIGNMENTS

Week of _____

Name:	○		○	
	○		○	
	○		○	
	○		○	

Name:	○		○	
	○		○	
	○		○	
	○		○	

Name:	○		○	
	○		○	
	○		○	
	○		○	

Videos WATCHED

Name:

Name:

Name:

Brainstorm

Weekly Plan

Week of _____

TO DO'S/*Notes*

_____
_____
_____
_____
_____
_____
_____
_____
_____
_____

_____
_____
_____
_____
_____
_____
_____
_____
_____
_____

Goals

Projects

Weekly Curriculum Plan

Week of _____

MATH

NAME	MONDAY	TUESDAY	WEDNESDAY	THURSDAY	FRIDAY

SCIENCE

NAME	MONDAY	TUESDAY	WEDNESDAY	THURSDAY	FRIDAY

HISTORY

NAME	MONDAY	TUESDAY	WEDNESDAY	THURSDAY	FRIDAY

ENGLISH

NAME	MONDAY	TUESDAY	WEDNESDAY	THURSDAY	FRIDAY

NAME	MONDAY	TUESDAY	WEDNESDAY	THURSDAY	FRIDAY

NAME	MONDAY	TUESDAY	WEDNESDAY	THURSDAY	FRIDAY

NAME	MONDAY	TUESDAY	WEDNESDAY	THURSDAY	FRIDAY

NAME	MONDAY	TUESDAY	WEDNESDAY	THURSDAY	FRIDAY

Weekly ASSIGNMENTS

Week of _____

Name:	○	○
	○	○
	○	○
	○	○

Name:	○	○
	○	○
	○	○
	○	○

Name:	○	○
	○	○
	○	○
	○	○

Videos WATCHED

Name:

Name:

Name:

Brainstorm

Monthly Reading Register

STUDENT:

Book Title & Author:

- ○ _____
- ○ _____
- ○ _____

STUDENT:

Book Title & Author:

- ○ _____
- ○ _____
- ○ _____

STUDENT:

Book Title & Author:

- ○ _____
- ○ _____
- ○ _____

Monthly Recap & Notes

_____

_____

_____

_____

_____

_____

_____

_____

_____

_____

_____

_____

_____

_____

_____

_____

_____

MONTH   YEAR

SUNDAY	MONDAY	TUESDAY	WEDNESDAY

MONTH   YEAR

It takes a BIG HEART to teach little minds

THURSDAY	FRIDAY	SATURDAY	REMINDERS/NOTES
			○ _____ _____ _____ _____
			○ _____ _____ _____ _____
			○ _____ _____ _____ _____
			○ _____ _____ _____ _____
			○ _____ _____ _____ ○ _____ _____ _____ _____

Weekly Plan

Week of _____

TO DO'S/*Notes*

_____
_____
_____
_____
_____
_____
_____
_____
_____
_____

_____
_____
_____
_____
_____
_____
_____
_____
_____
_____
_____
_____

Goals

Projects

Weekly Curriculum Plan

Week of _____

MATH	NAME	MONDAY	TUESDAY	WEDNESDAY	THURSDAY	FRIDAY

SCIENCE	NAME	MONDAY	TUESDAY	WEDNESDAY	THURSDAY	FRIDAY

HISTORY	NAME	MONDAY	TUESDAY	WEDNESDAY	THURSDAY	FRIDAY

ENGLISH	NAME	MONDAY	TUESDAY	WEDNESDAY	THURSDAY	FRIDAY

	NAME	MONDAY	TUESDAY	WEDNESDAY	THURSDAY	FRIDAY

	NAME	MONDAY	TUESDAY	WEDNESDAY	THURSDAY	FRIDAY

	NAME	MONDAY	TUESDAY	WEDNESDAY	THURSDAY	FRIDAY

	NAME	MONDAY	TUESDAY	WEDNESDAY	THURSDAY	FRIDAY

Weekly ASSIGNMENTS

Week of _____

Name:	○	○
	○	○
	○	○
	○	○

Name:	○	○
	○	○
	○	○
	○	○

Name:	○	○
	○	○
	○	○
	○	○

Videos WATCHED

Name:

Name:

Name:

Brainstorm

Weekly Plan

Week of _____

TO DO'S/*Notes*

_____
_____
_____
_____
_____
_____
_____
_____
_____
_____
_____

_____
_____
_____
_____
_____
_____
_____
_____
_____
_____
_____
_____

Goals

Projects

Weekly Curriculum Plan

Week of _____

<table>
<tr><td rowspan="4">MATH</td><td>NAME</td><td>MONDAY</td><td>TUESDAY</td><td>WEDNESDAY</td><td>THURSDAY</td><td>FRIDAY</td></tr>
<tr><td></td><td></td><td></td><td></td><td></td><td></td></tr>
<tr><td></td><td></td><td></td><td></td><td></td><td></td></tr>
<tr><td></td><td></td><td></td><td></td><td></td><td></td></tr>
</table>

	NAME	MONDAY	TUESDAY	WEDNESDAY	THURSDAY	FRIDAY
SCIENCE						

	NAME	MONDAY	TUESDAY	WEDNESDAY	THURSDAY	FRIDAY
HISTORY						

	NAME	MONDAY	TUESDAY	WEDNESDAY	THURSDAY	FRIDAY
ENGLISH						

NAME	MONDAY	TUESDAY	WEDNESDAY	THURSDAY	FRIDAY

NAME	MONDAY	TUESDAY	WEDNESDAY	THURSDAY	FRIDAY

NAME	MONDAY	TUESDAY	WEDNESDAY	THURSDAY	FRIDAY

NAME	MONDAY	TUESDAY	WEDNESDAY	THURSDAY	FRIDAY

Weekly ASSIGNMENTS

Week of _____

Name:	○	○
	○	○
	○	○
	○	○

Name:	○	○
	○	○
	○	○
	○	○

Name:	○	○
	○	○
	○	○
	○	○

Videos WATCHED

Name:

Name:

Name:

Brainstorm

Weekly Plan

Week of _____

TO DO'S/*Notes*

_____
_____
_____
_____
_____
_____
_____
_____
_____
_____
_____

Goals

_____
_____
_____
_____
_____
_____
_____
_____
_____
_____
_____
_____
_____
_____

Projects

Weekly Curriculum Plan

Week of _____

MATH

NAME	MONDAY	TUESDAY	WEDNESDAY	THURSDAY	FRIDAY

SCIENCE

NAME	MONDAY	TUESDAY	WEDNESDAY	THURSDAY	FRIDAY

HISTORY

NAME	MONDAY	TUESDAY	WEDNESDAY	THURSDAY	FRIDAY

ENGLISH

NAME	MONDAY	TUESDAY	WEDNESDAY	THURSDAY	FRIDAY

NAME	MONDAY	TUESDAY	WEDNESDAY	THURSDAY	FRIDAY

NAME	MONDAY	TUESDAY	WEDNESDAY	THURSDAY	FRIDAY

NAME	MONDAY	TUESDAY	WEDNESDAY	THURSDAY	FRIDAY

NAME	MONDAY	TUESDAY	WEDNESDAY	THURSDAY	FRIDAY

Weekly ASSIGNMENTS

Week of ───────────────────

Name:	○	○
	○	○
	○	○
	○	○

Name:	○	○
	○	○
	○	○
	○	○

Name:	○	○
	○	○
	○	○
	○	○

Videos WATCHED

Name:

Name:

Name:

Brainstorm

Weekly Plan

Week of _____

TO DO'S/*Notes*

_____
_____
_____
_____
_____
_____
_____
_____
_____
_____
_____

_____
_____
_____
_____
_____
_____
_____
_____
_____
_____
_____

Goals

Projects

Weekly Curriculum Plan

Week of _____

MATH	NAME	MONDAY	TUESDAY	WEDNESDAY	THURSDAY	FRIDAY

SCIENCE	NAME	MONDAY	TUESDAY	WEDNESDAY	THURSDAY	FRIDAY

HISTORY	NAME	MONDAY	TUESDAY	WEDNESDAY	THURSDAY	FRIDAY

ENGLISH	NAME	MONDAY	TUESDAY	WEDNESDAY	THURSDAY	FRIDAY

NAME	MONDAY	TUESDAY	WEDNESDAY	THURSDAY	FRIDAY

NAME	MONDAY	TUESDAY	WEDNESDAY	THURSDAY	FRIDAY

NAME	MONDAY	TUESDAY	WEDNESDAY	THURSDAY	FRIDAY

NAME	MONDAY	TUESDAY	WEDNESDAY	THURSDAY	FRIDAY

Weekly ASSIGNMENTS

Week of _____

Name:	○		○	
	○		○	
	○		○	
	○		○	

Name:	○		○	
	○		○	
	○		○	
	○		○	

Name:	○		○	
	○		○	
	○		○	
	○		○	

Videos WATCHED

Name:

Name:

Name:

Brainstorm

Monthly Reading Register

STUDENT:

Book Title & Author:

○ _____

○ _____

○ _____

STUDENT:

Book Title & Author:

○ _____

○ _____

○ _____

STUDENT:

Book Title & Author:

○ _____

○ _____

○ _____

Monthly Recap & Notes

_____

_____

_____

_____

_____

_____

_____

_____

_____

_____

_____

_____

_____

_____

_____

_____

MONTH

YEAR

SUNDAY	MONDAY	TUESDAY	WEDNESDAY

MONTH

YEAR

It takes a BIG HEART to teach little minds

THURSDAY	FRIDAY	SATURDAY	REMINDERS/NOTES
			○ _____ _____ _____ _____
			○ _____ _____ _____ _____
			○ _____ _____ _____
			○ _____ _____ _____ _____
			○ _____ _____ _____ ○ _____ _____ _____ _____

Weekly Plan

Week of _____

TO DO'S/*Notes*

_____
_____
_____
_____
_____
_____
_____
_____
_____
_____
_____

_____
_____
_____
_____
_____
_____
_____
_____
_____
_____
_____

Goals

Projects

Weekly Curriculum Plan

Week of _____

MATH

NAME	MONDAY	TUESDAY	WEDNESDAY	THURSDAY	FRIDAY

SCIENCE

NAME	MONDAY	TUESDAY	WEDNESDAY	THURSDAY	FRIDAY

HISTORY

NAME	MONDAY	TUESDAY	WEDNESDAY	THURSDAY	FRIDAY

ENGLISH

NAME	MONDAY	TUESDAY	WEDNESDAY	THURSDAY	FRIDAY

NAME	MONDAY	TUESDAY	WEDNESDAY	THURSDAY	FRIDAY

NAME	MONDAY	TUESDAY	WEDNESDAY	THURSDAY	FRIDAY

NAME	MONDAY	TUESDAY	WEDNESDAY	THURSDAY	FRIDAY

NAME	MONDAY	TUESDAY	WEDNESDAY	THURSDAY	FRIDAY

Weekly ASSIGNMENTS

Week of _____

Name:	○	○
	○	○
	○	○
	○	○

Name:	○	○
	○	○
	○	○
	○	○

Name:	○	○
	○	○
	○	○
	○	○

Videos WATCHED

Name:

Name:

Name:

Brainstorm

Weekly Plan

Week of _____

TO DO'S/*Notes*

_____
_____
_____
_____
_____
_____
_____
_____
_____
_____

_____
_____
_____
_____
_____
_____
_____
_____
_____
_____

Goals

Projects

Weekly Curriculum Plan

Week of _____

MATH

NAME	MONDAY	TUESDAY	WEDNESDAY	THURSDAY	FRIDAY

SCIENCE

NAME	MONDAY	TUESDAY	WEDNESDAY	THURSDAY	FRIDAY

HISTORY

NAME	MONDAY	TUESDAY	WEDNESDAY	THURSDAY	FRIDAY

ENGLISH

NAME	MONDAY	TUESDAY	WEDNESDAY	THURSDAY	FRIDAY

NAME	MONDAY	TUESDAY	WEDNESDAY	THURSDAY	FRIDAY

NAME	MONDAY	TUESDAY	WEDNESDAY	THURSDAY	FRIDAY

NAME	MONDAY	TUESDAY	WEDNESDAY	THURSDAY	FRIDAY

NAME	MONDAY	TUESDAY	WEDNESDAY	THURSDAY	FRIDAY

Weekly ASSIGNMENTS

Week of _____

Name:	○		○	
	○		○	
	○		○	
	○		○	

Name:	○		○	
	○		○	
	○		○	
	○		○	

Name:	○		○	
	○		○	
	○		○	
	○		○	

Videos WATCHED

Name:

Name:

Name:

Brainstorm

Weekly Plan

Week of _____

TO DO'S/*Notes*

_____
_____
_____
_____
_____
_____
_____
_____
_____
_____

_____
_____
_____
_____
_____
_____
_____
_____
_____
_____

Goals

Projects

Weekly Curriculum Plan

Week of _____

<table>
<tr><th>MATH</th><th>NAME</th><th>MONDAY</th><th>TUESDAY</th><th>WEDNESDAY</th><th>THURSDAY</th><th>FRIDAY</th></tr>
<tr><td></td><td></td><td></td><td></td><td></td><td></td><td></td></tr>
<tr><td></td><td></td><td></td><td></td><td></td><td></td><td></td></tr>
<tr><td></td><td></td><td></td><td></td><td></td><td></td><td></td></tr>
</table>

SCIENCE	NAME	MONDAY	TUESDAY	WEDNESDAY	THURSDAY	FRIDAY

HISTORY	NAME	MONDAY	TUESDAY	WEDNESDAY	THURSDAY	FRIDAY

ENGLISH	NAME	MONDAY	TUESDAY	WEDNESDAY	THURSDAY	FRIDAY

	NAME	MONDAY	TUESDAY	WEDNESDAY	THURSDAY	FRIDAY

	NAME	MONDAY	TUESDAY	WEDNESDAY	THURSDAY	FRIDAY

	NAME	MONDAY	TUESDAY	WEDNESDAY	THURSDAY	FRIDAY

	NAME	MONDAY	TUESDAY	WEDNESDAY	THURSDAY	FRIDAY

Weekly ASSIGNMENTS

Week of _____

Name:	○		○	
	○		○	
	○		○	
	○		○	

Name:	○		○	
	○		○	
	○		○	
	○		○	

Name:	○		○	
	○		○	
	○		○	
	○		○	

Videos WATCHED

Name:

Name:

Name:

Brainstorm

Weekly Plan

Week of _____

TO DO'S/*Notes*

_____
_____
_____
_____
_____
_____
_____
_____
_____

_____
_____
_____
_____
_____
_____
_____
_____
_____

Goals

Projects

Weekly Curriculum Plan

Week of _____

MATH	NAME	MONDAY	TUESDAY	WEDNESDAY	THURSDAY	FRIDAY

SCIENCE	NAME	MONDAY	TUESDAY	WEDNESDAY	THURSDAY	FRIDAY

HISTORY	NAME	MONDAY	TUESDAY	WEDNESDAY	THURSDAY	FRIDAY

ENGLISH	NAME	MONDAY	TUESDAY	WEDNESDAY	THURSDAY	FRIDAY

NAME	MONDAY	TUESDAY	WEDNESDAY	THURSDAY	FRIDAY

NAME	MONDAY	TUESDAY	WEDNESDAY	THURSDAY	FRIDAY

NAME	MONDAY	TUESDAY	WEDNESDAY	THURSDAY	FRIDAY

NAME	MONDAY	TUESDAY	WEDNESDAY	THURSDAY	FRIDAY

Weekly ASSIGNMENTS

Week of _____

Name:	○	○
	○	○
	○	○
	○	○

Name:	○	○
	○	○
	○	○
	○	○

Name:	○	○
	○	○
	○	○
	○	○

Videos WATCHED

Name:

Name:

Name:

Brainstorm

Monthly Reading Register

STUDENT:

Book Title & Author:

○ _____

○ _____

○ _____

STUDENT:

Book Title & Author:

○ _____

○ _____

○ _____

STUDENT:

Book Title & Author:

○ _____

○ _____

○ _____

Monthly Recap & Notes

_____
_____
_____
_____
_____
_____
_____
_____
_____
_____
_____
_____
_____
_____
_____
_____
_____

MONTH   YEAR

SUNDAY	MONDAY	TUESDAY	WEDNESDAY

It takes a BIG HEART to teach little minds

THURSDAY	FRIDAY	SATURDAY	REMINDERS/NOTES
			○ _____ _____ _____ _____
			○ _____ _____ _____ _____
			○ _____ _____ _____
			○ _____ _____ _____
			○ _____ _____ ○ _____ _____ _____ _____

Weekly Plan

Week of _____

TO DO'S/*Notes*

_____
_____
_____
_____
_____
_____
_____
_____
_____
_____

_____
_____
_____
_____
_____
_____
_____
_____
_____
_____

Goals

Projects

Weekly Curriculum Plan

Week of _____

	NAME	MONDAY	TUESDAY	WEDNESDAY	THURSDAY	FRIDAY
MATH						

	NAME	MONDAY	TUESDAY	WEDNESDAY	THURSDAY	FRIDAY
SCIENCE						

	NAME	MONDAY	TUESDAY	WEDNESDAY	THURSDAY	FRIDAY
HISTORY						

	NAME	MONDAY	TUESDAY	WEDNESDAY	THURSDAY	FRIDAY
ENGLISH						

NAME	MONDAY	TUESDAY	WEDNESDAY	THURSDAY	FRIDAY

NAME	MONDAY	TUESDAY	WEDNESDAY	THURSDAY	FRIDAY

NAME	MONDAY	TUESDAY	WEDNESDAY	THURSDAY	FRIDAY

NAME	MONDAY	TUESDAY	WEDNESDAY	THURSDAY	FRIDAY

Weekly ASSIGNMENTS

Week of _____

Name:	○		○	
	○		○	
	○		○	
	○		○	

Name:	○		○	
	○		○	
	○		○	
	○		○	

Name:	○		○	
	○		○	
	○		○	
	○		○	

Videos WATCHED

Name:

Name:

Name:

Brainstorm

Weekly Plan

Week of _____

TO DO'S/*Notes*

_____
_____
_____
_____
_____
_____
_____
_____
_____
_____

_____
_____
_____
_____
_____
_____
_____
_____
_____
_____
_____
_____

Goals

Projects

Weekly Curriculum Plan

Week of _____

	NAME	MONDAY	TUESDAY	WEDNESDAY	THURSDAY	FRIDAY
MATH						

	NAME	MONDAY	TUESDAY	WEDNESDAY	THURSDAY	FRIDAY
SCIENCE						

	NAME	MONDAY	TUESDAY	WEDNESDAY	THURSDAY	FRIDAY
HISTORY						

	NAME	MONDAY	TUESDAY	WEDNESDAY	THURSDAY	FRIDAY
ENGLISH						

NAME	MONDAY	TUESDAY	WEDNESDAY	THURSDAY	FRIDAY

NAME	MONDAY	TUESDAY	WEDNESDAY	THURSDAY	FRIDAY

NAME	MONDAY	TUESDAY	WEDNESDAY	THURSDAY	FRIDAY

NAME	MONDAY	TUESDAY	WEDNESDAY	THURSDAY	FRIDAY

Weekly ASSIGNMENTS

Week of _____

Name:	○	○
	○	○
	○	○
	○	○

Name:	○	○
	○	○
	○	○
	○	○

Name:	○	○
	○	○
	○	○
	○	○

Videos WATCHED

Name:

Name:

Name:

Brainstorm

Weekly Plan

Week of _____

TO DO'S/*Notes*

_____
_____
_____
_____
_____
_____
_____
_____
_____
_____

_____
_____
_____
_____
_____
_____
_____
_____
_____
_____
_____

Goals

Projects

Weekly Curriculum Plan

Week of _____

	NAME	MONDAY	TUESDAY	WEDNESDAY	THURSDAY	FRIDAY
MATH						

	NAME	MONDAY	TUESDAY	WEDNESDAY	THURSDAY	FRIDAY
SCIENCE						

	NAME	MONDAY	TUESDAY	WEDNESDAY	THURSDAY	FRIDAY
HISTORY						

	NAME	MONDAY	TUESDAY	WEDNESDAY	THURSDAY	FRIDAY
ENGLISH						

NAME	MONDAY	TUESDAY	WEDNESDAY	THURSDAY	FRIDAY

NAME	MONDAY	TUESDAY	WEDNESDAY	THURSDAY	FRIDAY

NAME	MONDAY	TUESDAY	WEDNESDAY	THURSDAY	FRIDAY

NAME	MONDAY	TUESDAY	WEDNESDAY	THURSDAY	FRIDAY

Weekly ASSIGNMENTS

Week of _____

Name:	○	○
	○	○
	○	○
	○	○

Name:	○	○
	○	○
	○	○
	○	○

Name:	○	○
	○	○
	○	○
	○	○

Videos WATCHED

Name:

Name:

Name:

Brainstorm

Weekly Plan

Week of _____

TO DO'S/*Notes*

_____

_____

_____

_____

_____

_____

_____

_____

_____

_____

_____

_____

_____

_____

_____

_____

_____

_____

_____

_____

_____

Goals

Projects

222

Weekly Curriculum Plan

Week of _____

MATH

NAME	MONDAY	TUESDAY	WEDNESDAY	THURSDAY	FRIDAY

SCIENCE

NAME	MONDAY	TUESDAY	WEDNESDAY	THURSDAY	FRIDAY

HISTORY

NAME	MONDAY	TUESDAY	WEDNESDAY	THURSDAY	FRIDAY

ENGLISH

NAME	MONDAY	TUESDAY	WEDNESDAY	THURSDAY	FRIDAY

NAME	MONDAY	TUESDAY	WEDNESDAY	THURSDAY	FRIDAY

NAME	MONDAY	TUESDAY	WEDNESDAY	THURSDAY	FRIDAY

NAME	MONDAY	TUESDAY	WEDNESDAY	THURSDAY	FRIDAY

NAME	MONDAY	TUESDAY	WEDNESDAY	THURSDAY	FRIDAY

Weekly ASSIGNMENTS

Week of _____

Name:	○		○	
	○		○	
	○		○	
	○		○	

Name:	○		○	
	○		○	
	○		○	
	○		○	

Name:	○		○	
	○		○	
	○		○	
	○		○	

Videos WATCHED

Name:

Name:

Name:

Brainstorm

Monthly Reading Register

STUDENT:

Book Title & Author:

- ○ _____
- ○ _____
- ○ _____

STUDENT:

Book Title & Author:

- ○ _____
- ○ _____
- ○ _____

STUDENT:

Book Title & Author:

- ○ _____
- ○ _____
- ○ _____

Monthly Recap & Notes

_____

_____

_____

_____

_____

_____

_____

_____

_____

_____

_____

_____

_____

_____

_____

_____

MONTH   YEAR

SUNDAY	MONDAY	TUESDAY	WEDNESDAY

MONTH   YEAR

It takes a BIG HEART to teach little minds

THURSDAY	FRIDAY	SATURDAY	REMINDERS/NOTES
			○ _____ _____ _____ _____
			○ _____ _____ _____ _____
			○ _____ _____ _____ _____
			○ _____ _____ _____ _____
			○ _____ _____ _____ ○ _____ _____ _____ _____

Weekly Plan

Week of _____

TO DO'S/*Notes*

_____
_____
_____
_____
_____
_____
_____
_____
_____
_____
_____

_____
_____
_____
_____
_____
_____
_____
_____
_____
_____
_____
_____

Goals

Projects

Weekly Curriculum Plan

Week of _____

<table>
<tr><td rowspan="4">MATH</td><td>NAME</td><td>MONDAY</td><td>TUESDAY</td><td>WEDNESDAY</td><td>THURSDAY</td><td>FRIDAY</td></tr>
<tr><td></td><td></td><td></td><td></td><td></td><td></td></tr>
<tr><td></td><td></td><td></td><td></td><td></td><td></td></tr>
<tr><td></td><td></td><td></td><td></td><td></td><td></td></tr>
</table>

<table>
<tr><td rowspan="4">SCIENCE</td><td>NAME</td><td>MONDAY</td><td>TUESDAY</td><td>WEDNESDAY</td><td>THURSDAY</td><td>FRIDAY</td></tr>
<tr><td></td><td></td><td></td><td></td><td></td><td></td></tr>
<tr><td></td><td></td><td></td><td></td><td></td><td></td></tr>
<tr><td></td><td></td><td></td><td></td><td></td><td></td></tr>
</table>

<table>
<tr><td rowspan="4">HISTORY</td><td>NAME</td><td>MONDAY</td><td>TUESDAY</td><td>WEDNESDAY</td><td>THURSDAY</td><td>FRIDAY</td></tr>
<tr><td></td><td></td><td></td><td></td><td></td><td></td></tr>
<tr><td></td><td></td><td></td><td></td><td></td><td></td></tr>
<tr><td></td><td></td><td></td><td></td><td></td><td></td></tr>
</table>

<table>
<tr><td rowspan="4">ENGLISH</td><td>NAME</td><td>MONDAY</td><td>TUESDAY</td><td>WEDNESDAY</td><td>THURSDAY</td><td>FRIDAY</td></tr>
<tr><td></td><td></td><td></td><td></td><td></td><td></td></tr>
<tr><td></td><td></td><td></td><td></td><td></td><td></td></tr>
<tr><td></td><td></td><td></td><td></td><td></td><td></td></tr>
</table>

<table>
<tr><td>NAME</td><td>MONDAY</td><td>TUESDAY</td><td>WEDNESDAY</td><td>THURSDAY</td><td>FRIDAY</td></tr>
<tr><td></td><td></td><td></td><td></td><td></td><td></td></tr>
<tr><td></td><td></td><td></td><td></td><td></td><td></td></tr>
<tr><td></td><td></td><td></td><td></td><td></td><td></td></tr>
</table>

<table>
<tr><td>NAME</td><td>MONDAY</td><td>TUESDAY</td><td>WEDNESDAY</td><td>THURSDAY</td><td>FRIDAY</td></tr>
<tr><td></td><td></td><td></td><td></td><td></td><td></td></tr>
<tr><td></td><td></td><td></td><td></td><td></td><td></td></tr>
<tr><td></td><td></td><td></td><td></td><td></td><td></td></tr>
</table>

<table>
<tr><td>NAME</td><td>MONDAY</td><td>TUESDAY</td><td>WEDNESDAY</td><td>THURSDAY</td><td>FRIDAY</td></tr>
<tr><td></td><td></td><td></td><td></td><td></td><td></td></tr>
<tr><td></td><td></td><td></td><td></td><td></td><td></td></tr>
<tr><td></td><td></td><td></td><td></td><td></td><td></td></tr>
</table>

<table>
<tr><td>NAME</td><td>MONDAY</td><td>TUESDAY</td><td>WEDNESDAY</td><td>THURSDAY</td><td>FRIDAY</td></tr>
<tr><td></td><td></td><td></td><td></td><td></td><td></td></tr>
<tr><td></td><td></td><td></td><td></td><td></td><td></td></tr>
<tr><td></td><td></td><td></td><td></td><td></td><td></td></tr>
</table>

Weekly ASSIGNMENTS

Week of _____

Name:	○	○
	○	○
	○	○
	○	○

Name:	○	○
	○	○
	○	○
	○	○

Name:	○	○
	○	○
	○	○
	○	○

Videos WATCHED

Name:

Name:

Name:

Brainstorm

Weekly Plan

Week of _____

TO DO'S/*Notes*

_____
_____
_____
_____
_____
_____
_____
_____
_____
_____

_____
_____
_____
_____
_____
_____
_____
_____
_____
_____

Goals

Projects

Weekly Curriculum Plan

Week of _____

MATH

NAME	MONDAY	TUESDAY	WEDNESDAY	THURSDAY	FRIDAY

NAME	MONDAY	TUESDAY	WEDNESDAY	THURSDAY	FRIDAY

NAME	MONDAY	TUESDAY	WEDNESDAY	THURSDAY	FRIDAY

NAME	MONDAY	TUESDAY	WEDNESDAY	THURSDAY	FRIDAY

NAME	MONDAY	TUESDAY	WEDNESDAY	THURSDAY	FRIDAY

NAME	MONDAY	TUESDAY	WEDNESDAY	THURSDAY	FRIDAY

NAME	MONDAY	TUESDAY	WEDNESDAY	THURSDAY	FRIDAY

NAME	MONDAY	TUESDAY	WEDNESDAY	THURSDAY	FRIDAY

Labels along left side: MATH, SCIENCE, HISTORY, ENGLISH

Weekly ASSIGNMENTS

Week of _____

Name:	○	○
	○	○
	○	○
	○	○

Name:	○	○
	○	○
	○	○
	○	○

Name:	○	○
	○	○
	○	○
	○	○

Videos WATCHED

Name:

Name:

Name:

Brainstorm

Weekly Plan

Week of _____

TO DO'S/*Notes*

_____
_____
_____
_____
_____
_____
_____
_____
_____
_____
_____

_____
_____
_____
_____
_____
_____
_____
_____
_____
_____
_____

Goals

Projects

Weekly Curriculum Plan

Week of _____

	NAME	MONDAY	TUESDAY	WEDNESDAY	THURSDAY	FRIDAY
MATH						

	NAME	MONDAY	TUESDAY	WEDNESDAY	THURSDAY	FRIDAY
SCIENCE						

	NAME	MONDAY	TUESDAY	WEDNESDAY	THURSDAY	FRIDAY
HISTORY						

	NAME	MONDAY	TUESDAY	WEDNESDAY	THURSDAY	FRIDAY
ENGLISH						

NAME	MONDAY	TUESDAY	WEDNESDAY	THURSDAY	FRIDAY

NAME	MONDAY	TUESDAY	WEDNESDAY	THURSDAY	FRIDAY

NAME	MONDAY	TUESDAY	WEDNESDAY	THURSDAY	FRIDAY

NAME	MONDAY	TUESDAY	WEDNESDAY	THURSDAY	FRIDAY

Weekly ASSIGNMENTS

Week of _____

Name:	○		○	
	○		○	
	○		○	
	○		○	

Name:	○		○	
	○		○	
	○		○	
	○		○	

Name:	○		○	
	○		○	
	○		○	
	○		○	

Videos WATCHED

Name:

Name:

Name:

Brainstorm

Weekly Plan

Week of _____

TO DO'S/*Notes*

_____
_____
_____
_____
_____
_____
_____
_____
_____
_____

Goals

_____
_____
_____
_____
_____
_____
_____
_____
_____
_____
_____
_____

Projects

Weekly Curriculum Plan

Week of _____

MATH

NAME	MONDAY	TUESDAY	WEDNESDAY	THURSDAY	FRIDAY

SCIENCE

NAME	MONDAY	TUESDAY	WEDNESDAY	THURSDAY	FRIDAY

HISTORY

NAME	MONDAY	TUESDAY	WEDNESDAY	THURSDAY	FRIDAY

ENGLISH

NAME	MONDAY	TUESDAY	WEDNESDAY	THURSDAY	FRIDAY

NAME	MONDAY	TUESDAY	WEDNESDAY	THURSDAY	FRIDAY

NAME	MONDAY	TUESDAY	WEDNESDAY	THURSDAY	FRIDAY

NAME	MONDAY	TUESDAY	WEDNESDAY	THURSDAY	FRIDAY

NAME	MONDAY	TUESDAY	WEDNESDAY	THURSDAY	FRIDAY

Weekly ASSIGNMENTS

Week of _____

Name:	○		○	
	○		○	
	○		○	
	○		○	

Name:	○		○	
	○		○	
	○		○	
	○		○	

Name:	○		○	
	○		○	
	○		○	
	○		○	

Videos WATCHED

Name:

Name:

Name:

Brainstorm

Monthly Reading Register

STUDENT:

Book Title & Author:

○ _____

○ _____

○ _____

STUDENT:

Book Title & Author:

○ _____

○ _____

○ _____

STUDENT:

Book Title & Author:

○ _____

○ _____

○ _____

Monthly Recap & Notes

MONTH

YEAR

SUNDAY	MONDAY	TUESDAY	WEDNESDAY

MONTH

YEAR

It takes a BIG HEART to teach little minds

THURSDAY	FRIDAY	SATURDAY	REMINDERS/NOTES
			○ _____ _____ _____ _____
			○ _____ _____ _____ _____
			○ _____ _____ _____ _____
			○ _____ _____ _____ _____
			○ _____ _____ _____ ○ _____ _____ _____ _____

Weekly Plan

Week of _____

TO DO'S/*Notes*

_____
_____
_____
_____
_____
_____
_____
_____
_____

_____
_____
_____
_____
_____
_____
_____
_____
_____

Goals

Projects

Weekly Curriculum Plan

Week of _____

	NAME	MONDAY	TUESDAY	WEDNESDAY	THURSDAY	FRIDAY
MATH						

	NAME	MONDAY	TUESDAY	WEDNESDAY	THURSDAY	FRIDAY
SCIENCE						

	NAME	MONDAY	TUESDAY	WEDNESDAY	THURSDAY	FRIDAY
HISTORY						

	NAME	MONDAY	TUESDAY	WEDNESDAY	THURSDAY	FRIDAY
ENGLISH						

NAME	MONDAY	TUESDAY	WEDNESDAY	THURSDAY	FRIDAY

NAME	MONDAY	TUESDAY	WEDNESDAY	THURSDAY	FRIDAY

NAME	MONDAY	TUESDAY	WEDNESDAY	THURSDAY	FRIDAY

NAME	MONDAY	TUESDAY	WEDNESDAY	THURSDAY	FRIDAY

Weekly ASSIGNMENTS

Week of _____

Name:	○	○
	○	○
	○	○
	○	○

Name:	○	○
	○	○
	○	○
	○	○

Name:	○	○
	○	○
	○	○
	○	○

Videos WATCHED

Name:

Name:

Name:

Brainstorm

Weekly Plan

Week of _____

TO DO'S/*Notes*

_____
_____
_____
_____
_____
_____
_____
_____
_____
_____
_____

Goals

_____
_____
_____
_____
_____
_____
_____
_____
_____
_____
_____
_____
_____
_____
_____
_____

Projects

Weekly Curriculum Plan

Week of _____

	NAME	MONDAY	TUESDAY	WEDNESDAY	THURSDAY	FRIDAY
MATH						

	NAME	MONDAY	TUESDAY	WEDNESDAY	THURSDAY	FRIDAY
SCIENCE						

	NAME	MONDAY	TUESDAY	WEDNESDAY	THURSDAY	FRIDAY
HISTORY						

	NAME	MONDAY	TUESDAY	WEDNESDAY	THURSDAY	FRIDAY
ENGLISH						

NAME	MONDAY	TUESDAY	WEDNESDAY	THURSDAY	FRIDAY

NAME	MONDAY	TUESDAY	WEDNESDAY	THURSDAY	FRIDAY

NAME	MONDAY	TUESDAY	WEDNESDAY	THURSDAY	FRIDAY

NAME	MONDAY	TUESDAY	WEDNESDAY	THURSDAY	FRIDAY

Weekly ASSIGNMENTS

Week of _____

Name:	○	○
	○	○
	○	○
	○	○

Name:	○	○
	○	○
	○	○
	○	○

Name:	○	○
	○	○
	○	○
	○	○

Videos WATCHED

Name:

Name:

Name:

Brainstorm

Weekly Plan

Week of _____

TO DO'S/*Notes*

_____
_____
_____
_____
_____
_____
_____
_____
_____
_____

_____
_____
_____
_____
_____
_____
_____
_____
_____
_____
_____

Goals

Projects

Weekly Curriculum Plan

Week of _____

	NAME	MONDAY	TUESDAY	WEDNESDAY	THURSDAY	FRIDAY
MATH						

	NAME	MONDAY	TUESDAY	WEDNESDAY	THURSDAY	FRIDAY
SCIENCE						

	NAME	MONDAY	TUESDAY	WEDNESDAY	THURSDAY	FRIDAY
HISTORY						

	NAME	MONDAY	TUESDAY	WEDNESDAY	THURSDAY	FRIDAY
ENGLISH						

NAME	MONDAY	TUESDAY	WEDNESDAY	THURSDAY	FRIDAY

NAME	MONDAY	TUESDAY	WEDNESDAY	THURSDAY	FRIDAY

NAME	MONDAY	TUESDAY	WEDNESDAY	THURSDAY	FRIDAY

NAME	MONDAY	TUESDAY	WEDNESDAY	THURSDAY	FRIDAY

Weekly ASSIGNMENTS

Week of _____

Name:	○	○
	○	○
	○	○
	○	○

Name:	○	○
	○	○
	○	○
	○	○

Name:	○	○
	○	○
	○	○
	○	○

Videos WATCHED

Name:

Name:

Name:

Brainstorm

Weekly Plan

Week of _____

TO DO'S/*Notes*

_____
_____
_____
_____
_____
_____
_____
_____
_____
_____

_____
_____
_____
_____
_____
_____
_____
_____
_____
_____

Goals

Projects

Weekly Curriculum Plan

Week of _____

MATH

NAME	MONDAY	TUESDAY	WEDNESDAY	THURSDAY	FRIDAY

SCIENCE

NAME	MONDAY	TUESDAY	WEDNESDAY	THURSDAY	FRIDAY

HISTORY

NAME	MONDAY	TUESDAY	WEDNESDAY	THURSDAY	FRIDAY

ENGLISH

NAME	MONDAY	TUESDAY	WEDNESDAY	THURSDAY	FRIDAY

NAME	MONDAY	TUESDAY	WEDNESDAY	THURSDAY	FRIDAY

NAME	MONDAY	TUESDAY	WEDNESDAY	THURSDAY	FRIDAY

NAME	MONDAY	TUESDAY	WEDNESDAY	THURSDAY	FRIDAY

NAME	MONDAY	TUESDAY	WEDNESDAY	THURSDAY	FRIDAY

Weekly ASSIGNMENTS

Week of _____

Name:	○	○
	○	○
	○	○
	○	○

Name:	○	○
	○	○
	○	○
	○	○

Name:	○	○
	○	○
	○	○
	○	○

Videos WATCHED

Name:

Name:

Name:

Brainstorm

Monthly Reading Register

STUDENT:

Book Title & Author:

- ○ _____
- ○ _____
- ○ _____

STUDENT:

Book Title & Author:

- ○ _____
- ○ _____
- ○ _____

STUDENT:

Book Title & Author:

- ○ _____
- ○ _____
- ○ _____

Monthly Recap & Notes

_____
_____
_____
_____
_____
_____
_____
_____
_____
_____
_____
_____
_____
_____

ATTENDANCE REGISTER | *Semester 2*

Name: _____

	January	February	March	April	May	June
1						
2						
3						
4						
5						
6						
7						
8						
9						
10						
11						
12						
13						
14						
15						
16						
17						
18						
19						
20						
21						
22						
23						
24						
25						
26						
27						
28						
29						
30						
31						

GRADE REGISTER | *Semester 2*

Name: _____

Subject: _____

Date	Assignment	Points Possible	Points Achieved	Grade
		Semester 1 Grade		

Subject: _____

Date	Assignment	Points Possible	Points Achieved	Grade
		Semester 1 Grade		

GRADE REGISTER | *Semester 2*

Name: _____

Subject: _____

Date	Assignment	Points Possible	Points Achieved	Grade

| Semester 1 Grade | |

Subject: _____

Date	Assignment	Points Possible	Points Achieved	Grade

| Semester 1 Grade |

GRADE REGISTER | *Semester 2*

Name: _____

Subject: _____

Date	Assignment	Points Possible	Points Achieved	Grade
Semester 1 Grade				

Subject: _____

Date	Assignment	Points Possible	Points Achieved	Grade
Semester 1 Grade				

GRADE REGISTER | *Semester 2*

Name: _____

Subject: _____

Date	Assignment	Points Possible	Points Achieved	Grade
	Semester 1 Grade			

Subject: _____

Date	Assignment	Points Possible	Points Achieved	Grade
	Semester 1 Grade			

Final Grades

Child's Name: _____

SUBJECT	1ST SEMESTER	2ND SEMESTER	FINAL

NOTES

Year End Recap & Notes

Child's Name: _____

SUCCESSES:

_____
_____
_____
_____
_____

HABITS:

_____
_____
_____
_____
_____

CHARACTER:

_____
_____
_____
_____

WHAT CAN WE DO BETTER?

_____
_____
_____
_____

OTHER NOTES:

_____

ATTENDANCE REGISTER | Semester 2

Name: _____

	January	February	March	April	May	June
1						
2						
3						
4						
5						
6						
7						
8						
9						
10						
11						
12						
13						
14						
15						
16						
17						
18						
19						
20						
21						
22						
23						
24						
25						
26						
27						
28						
29						
30						
31						

GRADE REGISTER | *Semester 2*

Name: _____

Subject: _____

Date	Assignment	Points Possible	Points Achieved	Grade

Subject: _____

Date	Assignment	Points Possible	Points Achieved	Grade

Semester 1 Grade

Semester 1 Grade

GRADE REGISTER | Semester 2

Name: _____

Subject: _____

Date	Assignment	Points Possible	Points Achieved	Grade
Semester 1 Grade				

Subject: _____

Date	Assignment	Points Possible	Points Achieved	Grade
Semester 1 Grade				

GRADE REGISTER | Semester 2

Name: _____

Subject: _____

Date	Assignment	Points Possible	Points Achieved	Grade

Subject: _____

Date	Assignment	Points Possible	Points Achieved	Grade

Semester 1 Grade

Semester 1 Grade

GRADE REGISTER | *Semester 2*

Name: _____

Subject: _____

Date	Assignment	Points Possible	Points Achieved	Grade
Semester 1 Grade				

Subject: _____

Date	Assignment	Points Possible	Points Achieved	Grade
Semester 1 Grade				

Final Grades | Child's Name: _____

SUBJECT	1ST SEMESTER	2ND SEMESTER	FINAL

NOTES

Year End Recap & Notes

Child's Name: _____

SUCCESSES:

_____

_____

_____

_____

HABITS:

_____

_____

_____

_____

CHARACTER:

_____

_____

_____

_____

WHAT CAN WE DO BETTER?

_____

_____

_____

_____

OTHER NOTES:

_____

_____

ATTENDANCE REGISTER | Semester 2

Name: _____

	January	February	March	April	May	June
1						
2						
3						
4						
5						
6						
7						
8						
9						
10						
11						
12						
13						
14						
15						
16						
17						
18						
19						
20						
21						
22						
23						
24						
25						
26						
27						
28						
29						
30						
31						

GRADE REGISTER | *Semester 2*

Name: _____

Subject: _____

Date	Assignment	Points Possible	Points Achieved	Grade
	Semester 1 Grade			

Subject: _____

Date	Assignment	Points Possible	Points Achieved	Grade
	Semester 1 Grade			

GRADE REGISTER | *Semester 2*

Name: _____

Subject: _____

Date	Assignment	Points Possible	Points Achieved	Grade
Semester 1 Grade				

Subject: _____

Date	Assignment	Points Possible	Points Achieved	Grade
Semester 1 Grade				

GRADE REGISTER | *Semester 2*

Name: _____

Subject: _____

Date	Assignment	Points Possible	Points Achieved	Grade
Semester 1 Grade				

Subject: _____

Date	Assignment	Points Possible	Points Achieved	Grade
Semester 1 Grade				

GRADE REGISTER | *Semester 2*

Name: _____

Subject: _____

Date	Assignment	Points Possible	Points Achieved	Grade
Semester 1 Grade				

Subject: _____

Date	Assignment	Points Possible	Points Achieved	Grade
Semester 1 Grade				

Final Grades

Child's Name: _____

SUBJECT	1ST SEMESTER	2ND SEMESTER	FINAL

NOTES

Year End Recap & Notes

Child's Name: _____

SUCCESSES:

_____
_____
_____
_____
_____
_____

HABITS:

_____
_____
_____
_____
_____
_____

CHARACTER:

_____
_____
_____
_____
_____
_____

WHAT CAN WE DO BETTER?

_____
_____
_____
_____
_____

OTHER NOTES:

_____
_____

SOME CALL IT *chaos* WE CALL IT ›homeschool‹

YEAR END *Reflections for Me*

MY SUCCESSES:

_____

_____

_____

_____

_____

MY HABITS (good or bad):

_____

_____

_____

_____

_____

CHARACTER TRAITS I NEED TO WORK ON:

_____

_____

_____

_____

_____

WHAT CAN I DO BETTER?

_____

_____

_____

_____

_____

OTHER NOTES:

_____

_____

_____

You never fail until you quit trying

Notes

Next Year At A Glance

NOTES:

- _____
  _____

- _____
  _____

- _____
  _____

- _____
  _____

- _____
  _____

- _____
  _____

AUGUST

SEPTEMBER

OCTOBER

NOVEMBER

DECEMBER

JANUARY

GOAL

\# of weeks _____

\# of days _____

Next Year At A Glance

NOTES:

FEBRUARY

-

MARCH

-

APRIL

-

MAY

-

JUNE

-

JULY

-

GOAL

\# of weeks _____

\# of days _____

Ideas for Next Year

Made in the USA
Monee, IL
19 August 2022

11801658R00162